SHOOTING
LIBERALLY

SHOOTING LIBERALLY

A Gun Guide for Democrats & Independents in a Time of Political Division

Christopher Hurst

For permission requests, commercial orders, or media inquiries, please contact us at:

Kilimanjaro Kutembea Publishing
Wind River Associates, Inc.
through the web portal on the bottom of the first page at:

https://www.kutembeapublishing.com

Print Book ISBN: 978-0-578-36161-1
eBook ISBN: 978-0-578-28052-3

Printed in the United States of America
First Edition, May 15, 2022

Note that the information in this book contains topics and techniques that can be dangerous. Always follow all rules from the manufacturers of all weapons and accessories or ammunition fully, as well as all local, state, and federal laws at all times. This book is academic in nature, rather than an instructional study of social, political, and self-defense topics, and should never replace individual professional instruction and training. The author, publisher, and distributor disclaim all liability from loss, injury, or damage, personal or otherwise, resulting from the information and procedures in this book.

CONTENTS

President Trump's insurrection on the steps of the U.S. Capitol, January 6, 2021. Credit Michael Brochstein, ZUMA Wire, Alamy Live News

INTRODUCTION

I am a Democrat. I served as an elected member of the Washington State House of Representatives for 14 years. I am also an expert in the use and handling of all types of firearms. That is because I am also a retired 25-year veteran police detective. I ended my law enforcement career as the Commander of a 15-city Homicide & Violent Crimes Task Force. I participated in the serving of over 1,400 search warrants for most crimes you could think of, including child rape, kidnapping, violent assault, drugs, and murder. There are few tactical or shooting situations I have not seen first-hand.

Most of my friends are liberal, but I also try to get along with my more conservative friends, at least the ones who still talk to me. Many have broken off those relationships, even within families. I try to talk to everyone. Americans should be doing this right now, albeit a difficult task at times.

Many of my liberal or Democratic friends have come to me recently for some very odd advice. Some want to know more about firearms in general. They assume I know a lot about them, and I do. Some are more specific and ask what type of a gun they should get. Some are worried about other Americans having guns. They want to understand and assess the risk of their fellow countrymen being armed, especially after seeing the events on January 6, 2021.

Others are concerned that the U.S. is at risk of a second Civil War. They believe a gun might become necessary if a Trumpian dictatorship were to take over America. Former President Donald Trump and his supporters not only attempted to overturn our last election, but they are now working to restrict future free and fair elections. They support Trump's false claim that he did not overwhelmingly lose the election in 2020.

Despite many repeated false allegations, extensive investigations, and legal challenges, no voter fraud was detected. He lost the election by over seven million votes. (I fully recognize that not all voters who found Mr. Trump to be the most attractive candidate do not accept his argument that he actually won the 2020 election. When I say "Trumpian" or "Trumpists" in this book, I am not referring to all voters who have supported Mr. Trump at the polls. I am using that term as a shorthand way of referring to those people who insist that the election was corrupted by fraud, that the January 26, 2021, riot in Washington, D.C. was not an insurrection that attempted to overthrow the election, and that militancy is necessary to displace our existing government.)

Facts are not stopping some of Trump's supporters from arming themselves in preparation for taking over America. Their plans rely upon their opponents, liberals, Independents, and Democrats, not being armed and opposing them, not unlike what happened to the people of Germany in the 1930s. That mistake led to millions of Germans and over 60 million people being killed because of the nationalist regimes in Germany, Japan, and Italy. Many German citizens who were opposed to Hitler or who were deemed "undesirables" were exterminated in gas chambers and death camps. Six million Jews from throughout Europe were executed in the Holocaust simply because they were Jewish. Comparisons of then and now might sound extreme – but consider how seemingly low-key it all started.

Some of this interest in guns by liberals, Independents, and Democrats surprised me, but I see a clear trend in why people feel unsafe. There are three main reasons. First, people on the right already have guns, especially military assault-style weapons. Independents, liberals, and Democrats feel they may need to defend themselves with guns in their own homes. Second, over half of Americans today believe that a second Civil War is entirely possible, a chilling thought. People wish to acquire firearms for their protection in case we lose our democracy and enter a dictatorship without our legislative and judicial branches of government to protect us. Third, people want to support the resistance if a dictatorial regime rises. They want to fight or supply weapons for those fighting to restore our freedom.

The founders of America were concerned that a dictatorship, not unlike a repressive King and church/state government might someday arise here. They fled England to get away from one. That is what the Second Amendment to the United States Constitution is all about.

Asking about getting a gun, or what type of gun to get, indicates a decision level of significance for liberal folks. They have crossed over a line of thinking about owning a firearm in theory to needing more information. It is a turning point.

Most Americans, even those who already have guns, know too little about them and even less about shooting situations. This book will provide information about the state of gun ownership in America. It will explain using a firearm properly and safely. A person who reads, understands, and accepts the lessons in this book, will be far more informed than most American gun owners.

The initial firearm question, should I own a gun, is complex. The answer may be vastly different from what one expected. This book will even suggest other solutions besides firearms for home or self-defense.

Knowing the basics about firearms, safety, and killing is a practical necessity. Are we as unsafe as you or I might think? What will the future bring? As I replied to my friends so they could make informed decisions and proceed safely, I realized that many people needed the same information. That's what inspired this book.

Many of my conservative-leaning friends have met the concept of this book with a shock that liberals, Democrats, and communities of color might think of getting guns. They've always assumed that guns were entirely their domain. But the coming years will see liberals, Democrats, and communities of color making up most of the market for new gun sales in America.

Much of this book will be new to people who don't have guns. Some parts will be surprising. Some of it will, out of necessity, be shocking. I have seen plenty of people injured and dead from firearms. Guns, gunfights, and firearm injuries are nothing like you will ever see on TV, in a movie, or in a video game. Although I will omit the ghastliest details, some information will be necessary for you to fully understand the responsibilities of gun ownership and the effects of using a gun to kill someone.

We are the only gun-owning country in the world with such a deficit of expertise among gun owners. Some countries have high percentages of gun ownership, but only a fraction of the gun violence, accidents, murders, and shootings happening in America. Gun ownership does not need to make a society unsafe, but gun ignorance does.

This book is not intended to be overtly political, with one exception, and that is in case America must face fascism and new-era Nazis here in our country. WWII and Hitler taught us that you cannot negotiate with fascists or Nazis. They see attempts to have a dialog as a weakness to be exploited. They have no regard for any concept of public policy or collective well-being. They will never agree to share power with any other person or institution. These principles have not changed since the rise of Hitler, Mussolini, and Tojo, in Germany, Italy, and Japan prior to WWII. No civilized society should give them safe harbor. They will find none in this book.

Regarding other political views, I will make statements that some liberals will find offensive – for example, like it or not, Second Amendment rights are currently settled law in America. Further, firearm ownership is not necessarily dangerous in a free country. On the other hand, I will offend some conservatives who refuse to accept the fact that Trumpists attempted an insurrection to reverse the presidential election on January 6, 2021.

Much of this book is about people considering arming themselves and preparing a defense should others decide not to respect the majority rule and the lives and liberty of all citizens. January 6th taught us that we have enough national instability already. There is a current risk of unrest that can lead to more violence unless things change. As Americans, we are all in this together. In my opinion, we should treat our right-of-center friends and fellow countrymen with respect and calm deliberation, work hard for reconciliation, but plan for the risk of a storm on the horizon we can all foresee.

Independents, liberals, Democrats, and people of color safely arming themselves can provide a significant deterrent to the plans of some radical Trumpists to end our democratic republic. Trumpists will be much more reluctant to attempt a takeover if they face opposition. We have a chance to keep our democracy from failing. This is what our founding fathers had in mind when our country was formed. This is what the Second Amendment and our right to bear arms are for ---our defense against tyranny.

CHAPTER ONE

THE SECOND AMENDMENT ISN'T JUST FOR REDNECKS

The Second Amendment to the U.S. Constitution says:

A well-regulated Militia, being necessary to the security of a free State, the right of the people to keep and bear Arms, shall not be infringed.

The Second Amendment is part of the Bill of Rights, the first 10 amendments to the Constitution spelling out the rights of the citizens to keep their new government in check. The Second Amendment outlines the rights of the citizens to protect themselves against tyranny.

For years, scholars debated whether the right to bear arms was a personal, individual right, or whether it pertained only to the right to participate in a militia. In recent years, the Supreme Court has declared that right to be both individual and collective.

Besides purchasing firearms for serving in militias, purchasers may own firearms for personal protection, hunting, and recreation like shooting targets.

However, the Second Amendment is not absolute—for example, states may bar some people, such as felons or those committing domestic violence, from owning firearms. One of the most conservative justices on the United States Supreme Court, Justice Antonin Scalia, made this clear in a ruling on the Second Amendment.

Another federal law regulating firearms is the Brady Bill that Congress enacted after the assassination attempt against President Ronald Reagan. It requires licensed federal firearms dealers to hold a newly purchased weapon for a three-day cooling-off period while the dealer runs criminal records checks on the purchaser. That law also banned sales of certain "assault weapons," but that clause of the law has since expired.

A Republican political consultant in the Pacific Northwest where I live is a good friend. We agree on very few policies, but we have enjoyed the chess game of running campaigns against each other. Like us, political opponents in America need not be enemies, and that is something we both believe. Some years ago, he told me that if liberals were right about Donald Trump and his desire to be a dictator, then I should be happy that the Second Amendment is there so we could restore our democracy. It seemed kind of funny in 2015, but after January 6, 2021, it's not funny anymore.

Is a country more, or less safe with firearms? Yes, no, and not necessarily. Nearly all citizens of Switzerland have been trained to use firearms to defend their country. They have very little crime, misuse, or improper discharge of firearms because of their regulations, education, and training. Their laws predominately pertain to acquiring, not owning firearms. No permit is necessary for just owning a firearm. A permit is necessary to buy semi and fully automatic firearms. You do not need to list a reason for semi-automatic firearms purchases unless the purpose is other than sport-shooting, hunting, or collecting. Concealed carry permits are seldom allowed, as are permits for fully automatic weapons, silencers, and lasers. Hollow-point and soft-point ammunition may be sold over the counter for hunting only.

There is a long-standing practice of the Swiss participating in their national militia, and the Swiss keep these service rifles in their personal homes. The Swiss also have a strong tradition of hunting, and this also accounts for many firearms in the country. Prior to 2008, no firearms were even registered. In a 2019 referendum, Swiss voters opted to conform with European Union regulations that restrict the acquisition of semi-automatic firearms with high-capacity magazines, although citizens are allowed to obtain one of these permits if they promise they will show after five and ten years that they're members of a shooting club, or that they used the weapon at least once a year within that five- and ten-year period.

In 2017 we had 39,773 firearm deaths in America, roughly one in 8,000, while Switzerland only had 214, or roughly one in 40,000. The problem is more about how Americans possess guns rather than the fact that they do so at all.

If you choose to assert your Second Amendment right to own a firearm you can also choose to be a responsible gun owner. There is little reason that your firearm should ever fall into the hands of criminals or be misused by others in your home or community.

Some extreme conservatives have told me that African Americans with firearms, especially AR-15s, are terrorists, and this book is a bad idea because it teaches people whom they think should not possess guns about acquiring, possessing, and using guns. However, even though there has been staggering racial repression in America against minority communities over the decades, the basic protections and promises of our Constitution apply to all American citizens equally, not just to rednecks.

The "Stadtkirche" in Freudenstadt, destroyed in World War II, 1945, photo permission Stadtarchiv Freudenstadt, #2009020610044216.

CHAPTER TWO

THE NAZI SWINE

You might think I overstate my concerns that Trumpism presents a risk to American democracy, and that by extension, my statements about considering the use of the Second Amendment to protect our country against the possible threat of tyranny are overstated. Let me tell you a story that illustrates why and what I feel.

My wife and I recently dined with a dear friend who lives not far from us. Her name is Ingrid, and this is what she told us:

In 1941, Ingrid and her mother were walking down Kopen-icker Strasse (Street) in downtown Berlin, not far from their home. It was a bright but chilly day, so she was wearing her heavy coat to keep warm. As they were returning home from shopping at a local store, two trucks stopped, one on either side of the street, and soldiers jumped out with guns in hand. They began screaming and grabbing everyone wearing yellow stars on their coats and throwing them into the trucks. She was five years old, but the memory is so strongly seared into her mind that she can still remember it like it was yesterday. She will never forget that moment and the yellow cloth stars that Jews were required to wear on their clothing when they were out in public. Those victims were never seen again on the streets of Berlin.

She said that the soldiers allowed no discussion. They just grabbed people without warning. It happened so quickly that no one had a chance to resist. The sudden violence of this happening for the first, but not the last time, was stunning to all. No one could fight back. Those farther away fled as quickly as they could. People were scattering through the streets in every direction. She remembers that her mother grabbed her arm and ran, but her little legs could hardly keep up because her mother was pulling so hard and fast to escape. Ingrid was frightened because her grandfather was Jewish and had to wear the yellow star whenever he left their home. Ingrid's family was afraid that the Nazi soldiers would get them, and they too would be exterminated. Even in 1941, many people in Germany were fully aware of the concentration camps and what was happening in them. Her grandfather had to live with Ingrid's family because Jews were not allowed to have houses or apartments of their own.

One day at the beginning of 1944, the Nazis captured her grandfather and took him to a concentration camp where he was killed in the gas chambers. Her father was frightened. He knew that it was only a matter of time before they would all be killed. He took his family on the next train to a town that was 440 miles to the west of Berlin in the Black Forest. It was a town called Freudenstadt. They left with just the clothes on their backs and had other property sent later by train.

Ingrid turned ten years old just before the end of WWII. She felt that she had lived more than a lifetime under nationalist Nazi rule. Another vivid memory she told us was about walking home from school near the end of the war when American pilots were bombing and strafing the railway yards in Freudenstadt. She said she could always hear the planes coming. She and her friends would jump into the ditch to keep from being hit by bullets. She said that the American fighters flew so low to the ground that she could see the faces of the pilots as they made their bombing and strafing runs down the road to the railway station. After the planes left, the children would get back onto the road and go back to being kids again. They had become that accustomed to war.

As the allies approached their town, the Nazis called the town together and gave everyone 13 years old or older a gun and ordered them to all fight to the death for Hitler and his nationalist Nazi regime. As the American and French soldiers came near the town, they asked for the town to surrender so they could spare the life and property of everyone there. The Nazi soldiers refused and told the Americans that the citizens would all fight to the death. The town was shelled by the allies' artillery for three days. It was destroyed. Ingrid and the survivors were hiding in a cave near town and the Nazis still demanded that everyone die fighting for

Hitler. The people had had enough and felt that they were going to die anyway, so they just marched out of the cave together and surrendered to the Americans. The Nazi soldiers could not stop and kill them all. This was the end of the war for the people of Freudenstadt, and the Americans soon turned the captured town over to the French. Peace had finally come.

Ingrid was a very good student and happened to speak and write fluent French, English and of course, German. Shortly after the war, she got a job as a translator for the US Army. She later met and married an American soldier. He took her back to the United States, where she has lived the rest of her life.

She knows first-hand what happened when Hitler told the German people that he would make Germany a great country again. She saw these policies in place when nationalism became the driving public outcry in Germany. She saw what happened when racial policies divided and attacked individual groups of citizens. She saw what happened when the voting rights of the citizens were taken away.

She has also watched carefully what has been happening in America since Trump entered public politics. The speeches, attacks, and policies she sees are identical to those she heard from Hitler and the Nazi party in Germany in the 1930s and 1940s. I asked her what she thought of Trump, considering January 6, 2021. After thinking for a moment, she responded simply, and without a hit of irony: "Trump is a Nazi swine."

In the week before Christmas in 2021, there was a headline on CNN that read, "Trump uses anti-Semitic tropes to again criticize Jewish Americans." He stated that Jewish Americans were disloyal to Israel and to evangelical Christians in America. He said, "It's a very dangerous thing that's happening," when referring to American Jews. He called them out, not only for being Jewish but for being dangerous and disloyal. Similarly, on January 30, 1939,

Adolf Hitler, August 5, 1939, Ber-   Former President Trump,
lin, Germany, Keystone Pictures,   November 24, 2015, Myrtle
Alamy Images.   Beach, South Carolina, Richard
                                     Ellis photo, Alamy Images.

Hitler gave a national speech in which he stated that Jews were
a danger to internal German security because of their inherent
disloyalty. In 2017 after the Nazi and white supremacists rally in
Charlottesville, Virginia, Trump said there were, "Very fine people
on both sides" to which Barack Obama responded, "How hard is
it to say that Nazis are bad?" When Trump's insurrectionists and
white supremacists attacked the capital on January 6th, he again
called them "great people" and said that he "loved" them.

   Trump's own handpicked military Chief of Staff, General Mark
Milley, compared the attack on our capital on January 6[th,] to the
1933 attack on Germany's parliament building, which Hitler used
to justify his nationalist Nazi dictatorship taking complete power
in Germany. is quoted as saying, "This is a Reichstag moment,"
and went on to call it, "The gospel of the Fuhrer." The Reichstag
was the German national government building like our United

States Capitol. Once it was destroyed, Hitler made himself dictator, eliminated elections, and stopped counting votes, just like Trumpists tried to do on January 6th. Milley also stated that the supporters that Trump sent to destroy the capitol that day and to hang Vice-President Mike Pence and members of our Congress were the same as the "brownshirts in the streets," that Hitler had used at Nazi rallies. The "brown shirts" were the personal supporters of Hitler who went around Germany suppressing votes in elections, intimidating elected and government officials from counting legally cast votes, and terrifying citizens. They usually had banners, weapons, and flags to scare the population into accepting Hitler. With no one to stop them, Hitler took over.

It is important to point out that most Germans were not members of the Nazi Party. Hitler's dictatorship did not represent most of the German people. Nazis ruled through terror and intimidation.

Ingrid told me it is critical that her personal family story of the Holocaust be told and re-told as often as possible so future generations might never forget those events. Her generation is passing away, but the stories of this terrible time should never be forgotten.

My friend Ingrid, along with many others, are convinced that America is living in troubling times, and that what happened in the Nazi Germany of her youth almost happened here in America on January 6th, and still could come to pass.

Military assault-style firearms come in thousands of individual variations. They are not a single firearm. One here has a bipod attachment for stabilization and a laser sight, along with a scope on each.

CHAPTER THREE

A VISUAL BASIC SUMMARY OF FIREARMS & TERMS

In case you are unfamiliar with basic firearms terms, I am including this chapter near the front of the book so you can understand

17

the ones you might need to make sense of the following chapters. Many of the terms will make more sense when you look at the corresponding photographs that show some of them. If you are familiar with these terms, then just skip to the next chapter.

Action - the mechanism that fires a gun:

Single Action firearm - You must pull a hammer back and lock it in place to cock it prior to pulling the trigger to fire the weapon.

Double Action firearm– When you pull the trigger, the hammer comes back then drops the firing pin onto the bullet to fire the weapon in one motion, but you can pull the hammer back and lock it into place manually, prior to pulling the trigger, if you prefer.

Semi-Automatic –When you pull the trigger, the firearm loads a bullet in the chamber, pulls the hammer back, fires, and reloads the next bullet automatically, but it only shoots one bullet for each pull of the trigger. Some of these weapons have no visible hammer on the outside. If there is not a round in the chamber when you begin, you must pull on a lever at the side of the gun by the chamber to manually put the first round or shell in place to begin the process. This also cocks the gun for the first shot.

Fully-Automatic – Same as the semi-automatic, but the gun keeps firing with a single pull until all the bullets have been fired from the gun. Usually, these fire around eight bullets per second until they are gone. These seldom have a visible hammer on the outside.

Ammunition: People tend to use the terms "bullet," "cartridge," "shell," "rounds" and "case" interchangeably. This section will explain the difference between those terms.

Shell or Cartridge – The cylindrical container that holds the gun-powder, lead tip of the bullet, and primer. They are usually made of brass, but they can be made of steel, aluminum, plastic, or in the case of shotgun shells, paper.

Bullet – Projectile that is fired from a gun, usually made of lead, sometimes covered by copper, but can be steel. The lead tip of a cartridge that is expelled from a shell when a firearm is fired. Commonly, the entire cartridge and lead are called a bullet.

Primer--The chemical contact explosive that sparks when struck by a firing pin, igniting the gunpowder in a cartridge.

Centerfire – Bullets that have primer at the back of the shell, in the center, which is hit by the firing pin.

Rimfire – Bullets that have their primer material at the back of the shell just inside of the rim, so the firing pin hits the shell on the edge, instead of in the center.

Shotgun Rounds or Shells – A round means a shell or case. Shotgun ammunition is usually called a shell and handgun and rifle ammunition are usually called rounds.

Powder, Gunpowder – The compound that explodes in the shell so that expanding pressure forces the bullet out of the muzzle of the firearm. Different types burn or explode at different speeds. Handgun powder usually explodes much faster than rifle powder because they have shorter barrels.

Black Powder – The original gunpower that explodes and does not burn. It is much more unstable than modern gunpower and even static electricity can set it off.

Birdshot – Shotgun pellets that are small and are usually used for hunting birds.

Buckshot – Large shotgun pellets that are usually used for killing people or large game. Often there are nine .17 caliber pellets in a shell.

Aught (written as "0") – The size of some shotgun pellets.

Target Ammunition – Ammunition and bullets for shooting paper targets at a range. They are generally inexpensive and of poor quality. These often include lead slugs without copper covering or jackets.

Jacketed Bullets – Bullets that have a copper covering not extending over the lead tip.

Full Metal Jacket & Military (NATO) ammunition – This is generally military ammunition that complies with the North Atlantic Treaty Organization and Hauge Conventions prohibiting bullets that expand or cause too much damage when they hit a person. The copper covering covers the entire bullet.

Hollowpoint – Bullets that have a hole in the lead slug at the tip, so they expand when hitting an object.

Dum Dum – An older term for a bullet that is soft on the end and expands when it hits something, usually a person.

Slug – A large piece of lead that is fired out of a shotgun as a single piece as opposed to smaller lead or steel pellets.

Assault Weapon, Assault-style weapon – A broad term usually referring to a semi-automatic or fully-automatic firearm with a detachable magazine, a pistol grip, and sometimes other features such as a vertical forward grip (handle under the barrel), flash suppressor, or barrel shroud. Certain firearms are specified by name in some laws that restrict assault weapons in different jurisdictions. When the now-defunct Federal Assault Weapons Ban was passed in 1994, the U.S. Department of Justice said, "In general, assault weapons are semiautomatic firearms with a large magazine of ammunition that were designed and configured for rapid fire and combat use," but the commonly used definitions of assault weapons are under frequent debate and change all the time. Honestly, this term does not really mean much anymore as there are so many different firearms that might qualify these days. In common terms, it means what any particular person thinks it means, based on their vision of a military weapon of war.

Barrel - The tube of a firearm from which the bullet is expelled. The hole through the barrel is the bore.

Rifling: Grooves machined in a spiral into the inside of a bore that makes a fired bullet spin as it travels down the barrel.

Smooth Bore – A barrel with no rifling in the barrel. Few modern firearms (rifles and handguns) are made this way, but all shotguns have smooth bores.

Caliber - The size of the ammunition that a weapon is designed to shoot, as measured by the bullet's approximate diameter in inches in the United States, and in millimeters in other countries. In some instances, ammunition is described with additional terms, such as the year of its introduction (30/06) or the name of the designer (.30 Newton). In some countries, ammunition is also described in terms of the length of the cartridge case (7.62 x 63 mm).

Carbine – A short barrel rifle, often a military one.

Chamber, or Breach – The place where the entire bullet case or shell goes in a firearm so that it is in position to be fired when hit by the hammer; the position in the action that the bullet is fired from.

Cylinder – A round metal piece that holds the shells or bullets for a revolver, usually a handgun.

Firing Pin – A metal part of the hammer that hits a bullet, igniting the primer and setting off the explosion in the case or shell.

Gauge, as in 12-Gauge - Shotguns are classified by gauge, which is a measure related to the diameter of the smooth shotgun bore and the size of the shotshell designed for that bore. Common shotgun gauges are 10-gauge, 12-gauge, 16-gauge, 20-gauge, and 410-gauge. The smaller the gauge number, the larger the shotgun bore.

Hammer – The part of the action that is released by the trigger to cause the firing pin to hit the bullet to fire a firearm. It is spring-loaded. It moves with a significant force to drive the firing pin onto the bullet to cause it to explode.

Hang-fire – You fire the weapon, but the powder fails to fully ignite or there is a light charge of powder, and the bullet only travels a short distance down the barrel and stops and is jammed there. If a second round is fired, it can blow up the gun and seriously injure or kill the person firing the weapon. This danger is far greater with automatic weapons.

Magazine – The container for bullets in a firearm. This piece is either built into the firearm itself or is a separate piece, or clip, which is slipped into the firearm, usually at the bottom below the chamber.

Magnum – Just a made-up term to make a firearm seem more powerful than it looks or is. Its actual meaning is a bottle of wine that is twice the size of a normal one. A trade name.

Misfire – You pull the trigger, and the hammer comes down on the primer, but it fails to fire.

Musket – A smooth bore firearm, usually a long-barreled one. These were once common but are now rare.

Pistol – A small gun you can hold in your hand.

Revolver – A handgun that holds multiple bullets, usually five or six, in a round cylinder that rotates after each time you fire, moving the next bullet into position to be fired.

Rifle as opposed to Rifling – A rifle is a long gun designed to be shot from the shoulder, as opposed to a shorter handgun shot from the hand. Most people today call all long firearms except shotguns rifles, even if they do not have rifling cut into the barrel.

Sighting In – To adjust the mechanical or optical scope on any firearm to assure that the scope is synchronized with the barrel, so the firearm is correctly aimed at the image visible in the scope.

Parts of a double-action six-shot revolver with a speed loader, in this case a Smith & Wesson Model 19 .357 Magnum that can also fire .38 Special rounds.

Cylinder Release

Hammer

Rear Sight

Front Sight

Muzzle

Barrel

Shell Ejector

6-Shot Cylinder

Trigger

Trigger Guard

Tactical Grip

.357 Bullet

Speed Loader

25

Parts of a semi-automatic hand gun, in this case a H&K that fires a .40 cal Smith & Wesson round.

Parts of a single-action six-shot revolver, in this case a Ruger .357 Magnum that also can fire .38 Special rounds.

Barrel

Front Sight

Muzzle

Magazine

Magazine Loading Port

ForeStock

Ejection Port

Rear Sight

Trigger Guard

Trigger

Safety

Grip

Stock

Shoulder Pad

Parts of a shotgun, in this case a Mossberg 590A1 Tactical pump-action model.

Parts of a typical single-shot bolt-action rifle with a scope, scope covers, and shoulder strap, in this case a Ruger .270 Winchester.

Additional parts of a typical rifle.

Special, as in .38 Special – Just another made-up word that infers something better than just a .38 caliber round of ammunition. A trade name.

Tactical – An encounter with another person, usually with firearms or a weapon, where the outcome has the risk of injury or death.

Trigger – The lever on the outside at the bottom of a firearm that you pull to fire the gun.

"Kill Jews" painted on a rock at a National Forest shooting location.

CHAPTER FOUR

WHO IS BUYING GUNS NOW, AND WHY?

Some years ago, a news story indicated that there were almost as many guns in America as there were Americans. That was a big story at the time, and today the number is higher. Although there is honestly no way to know for sure, most experts agree that there are somewhere around 1.2 guns per person in our country, or roughly 400 million guns.

There was a big upswing in purchases of guns and ammunition after the election of President Obama. Conservatives were concerned that he would attempt gun control. They bought so much ammunition that local Walmarts were unable to keep up with their customers' demand for ammo, even small caliber .22 shells. This panic tapered off over time. Alarmists failed to realize that President Obama was a trained Constitutional lawyer who knew the status of Second Amendment law.

The Supreme Court decision of *District of Columbia v. Heller* was announced in June 2008, six months before Obama took office. Before that time, the Court had not considered the ultimate question, "Is the right to bear arms an individual right?" Historically, the NRA and guns rights proponents didn't bring the case to court for fear that the Supreme Court of the United States would hold that the Second Amendment did NOT create an individual right to own firearms; and no gun control advocates filed the case for fear that the Court would hold that individual ownership WAS an individual right.

As a constitutional law professor, Obama undoubtedly was aware of this historical stand-off. Although there was panic buying of firearms and ammunition when he was elected, Obama did not promise or attempt to act on guns until he wept over the slaughter of the 6-year-olds at Sandy Hook, and said in essence, "Something should be done" but he never proposed any attempt to repeal the Second Amendment.

When Trump was elected, a rush to purchase firearms began again. This corresponded to an explosion in the purchase of "military-style assault weapons" (More on these firearms in Chapter

13). There were three reasons for this. First, a 10-year ban on sales of "assault weapons," enacted under President Reagan in 1994 had expired. Although it was debated at length, Congress did not reinstate the ban, so assault-style weapons became widely available. Second, people noticed these types of weapons and thought they were cool. Frequently, these weapons were purchased by poorly trained people who knew little about them, often, young white men.

Third, there were purchases by conservative Trumpists who are currently "training" with these weapons for what they see as the coming second American Civil War. They are convinced that liberals, Democrats, and communities of color will never consider doing anything similar, so when they do take over, they will receive a full and quick surrender. Their concept isn't so much to use firearms in combat as to use them to intimidate others into a quick political result.

You might be wondering how Trump supporters responded immediately after the insurrection on January 6, 2021. FBI data can give a bit of a look into the overall American response. Federal firearms background checks for gun purchases jumped 40% from 2020 to a staggering 12,452,319 checks in the first quarter of 2021. Many purchases these days are not reported, and these checks were not done, so not all purchases are even reflected in these numbers. This increase coincided with a significant shortage of ammunition on store shelves, especially for rounds of ammunition that can be fired from military assault-style weapons, like AR-15s. Some store shelves are bare, even today, and larger stores have placed limits on the number of boxes a customer may buy during one visit. Recently, the outdoor national retailer, Bass Pro, limited customers to 5 boxes of this type of ammunition, when it is available. A box contains 20 rounds (bullets). Equally impactful

Atomwaffen Division members in the forests of Washington State with their firearms.

is the cost. Not long ago, these rounds cost roughly $.30 each, but now usually sell for over a dollar, even for very poor-quality bullets made in Russia or China.

American manufacturers make over 12 billion rounds of ammunition per year, so this is not a supply chain or scarcity issue. This is consumer-driven by people hoarding bullets and preparing for political and civil strife in America. This is not an overstatement. In March of 2019, U.S. Representative Steve King, R-Iowa, posted a meme about a hypothetical civil war between "blue states" and "red states." The since-deleted post was an image of two figures composed of traditionally Democratic-leaning and Republican-leaning states in fighting postures with text over the top and a caption that read: "Folks keep talking about another civil war. One side has about 8 trillion bullets, while the other side doesn't know which bathroom to use."

This is not about shadowy messages hidden deep on the internet or elsewhere. This was a sitting United States Congressman publicly stating that he and his supporters were buying and storing bullets to kill Americans who did not agree with them in a second American Civil War, one that would usher in a Trumpian dictatorship and the end of our democratic republic. In 2018, when King's white supremacist views were already widely known, Trump campaigned with King and proudly said to a cheering crowd, "[King] may be the world's most conservative human being." Trump boasted that he had raised more campaign money for King than any other candidate that year. Fortunately, King was opposed by the Republican party and lost his primary in 2020. He is no longer in congress, but his views are a picture of how some Americans feel.

Moving forward, something entirely new is happening in America. The other day I ran into a good friend whom I hadn't seen in a while due to the pandemic. This woman and her husband are very progressive liberals. Both are college-educated, and she is a lawyer. As we were talking and catching up, I mentioned this book. After about five minutes, she went back to the subject of the book and said sheepishly that they both had bought guns for themselves. Being surprised and curious, I asked why. She told me it was a direct response to January 6, 2021, and the rise of Trumpism. Another very progressive liberal neighbor told me in February of 2022, that she plans to get an AR-15 sometime soon, for this very same reason.

This perceived threat from the events surrounding January 6, 2021, is beginning to drive a new group of gun buyers in America to do more than just plan, but to purchase firearms as well.

My friend Tommy Agiak in Kaktovik, Alaska, with a whale gun in 1984.

CHAPTER FIVE

A BRIEF HISTORY
OF FIREARMS

There is a fascinating principle in law called "Inevitable discovery." Simplified, it means that evidence discovered illegally

A whale gun fires this explosive bullet.

can still be used against an accused criminal in a trial if it would have been lawfully found someday anyway. A simple example is a dead body. A dead body will be discovered eventually, even if it is found illegally, say during police entry into a building with a warrant that turns out to be defective. Things that will be found anyway are just a reality, so must be addressed by society. We can't wish them away or pretend they do not exist.

Discoveries in science will inevitably be found as well. For better or worse, humans were always going to discover subatomic particles and in so doing, make atomic bombs and blow each other up. It was always going to happen. Throughout history, people have made discoveries that help them survive and live better, but they also have found ways to turn discoveries into weapons.

In roughly the ninth century, Chinese chemists mixed sulfur, charcoal, and saltpeter and found that when ignited, it blew up. This was early gunpowder, and after it was discovered, it made great fireworks. Then someone wondered what would happen if you compressed that explosion in a tube, added fragments of hard material, and shot it at someone else. Although crude, it was a firearm. Millions of people have been shot since then by all manner of devices that use gunpowder. It would have been nice if we had just stopped at fireworks, but human history has often been violent.

As technology advances, most inventions are succeeded by something new, but a few things never change much. Gunpower is one of them. Even modern explosives have not replaced age-old gunpowder in some of the most modern personal firearms in use today.

Firearms did not create wars, but they did make them less personal. Shooting someone a long distance off was much different from stabbing a person with a sword. Dropping bombs or shooting a cannon at others is much different from using a spear. Humans created efficiencies but also lessened the amount of personal courage necessary for combatants.

Some cultures, like the Samurai of ancient Japan, resisted these new modern weapons because they felt that more distant killing was not honorable. It's an interesting point. How many large wars would have been fought if the leaders and their families were required to be on the front lines of personal combat?

What was once largely a product for war also became useful in hunting. It's safer to kill a deer or a bear with a firearm than a spear, something that made feeding a family easier, before supermarkets.

It wasn't long ago that many Americans hunted with rifles or shotguns to put food on their tables. Some still do. Hunting for food requires some personal responsibility in harvesting it. It was not uncommon for some native cultures to return the hooves and bones of harvested creatures to the forest to show their thanks, and to prove that they had not wasted any of it. Such was the respect and obligation people felt when they were in tune with nature, a healthy process, and firearms were a part of it. Respectful and responsible hunting in America remains a part of our national history and culture.

At the time the Second Amendment was enacted, the firearms available for personal and military use were not even a fraction as powerful, accurate, or complex as the ones on the market today.

The muskets used in the American Revolution were highly inaccurate smooth-bore long guns. The rifling inside the barrels of guns (the valleys and ridges) which make them much more accurate, didn't become widely used until the 1800s. That was the dawn of modern firearms.

Most modern firearms today are lighter and far more accurate than older ones. Some can hold many bullets, rather than just one. Others can fire and reload bullets into their firing chambers automatically, allowing the shooter to fire many bullets per second. Semi-automatic and fully automatic firearms are widely available in America today, and many are in the hands of people who have no practical use or training for them. For these owners, their guns are more of a status symbol or political statement than a self-defense or hunting tool. Most of them are not good for hunting because they do too much damage to the meat or are far too inaccurate.

Recent American history of firearms saw social and political developments as well. In editing this book, a friend reminded me of a scene in a movie where the hero breaks into the wrong hotel room, one full of people. Everyone inside pulls out a gun and aims it at the hero all at once. The hero responds, "Oh, Americans." That is how the world sees Americans, and honestly, it's how we see ourselves these days. We know that this part of our image is an accurate assessment. Right or wrong, being the toughest kid on the block is part of being an American. Weapons and our military are part of how we project power on the world stage. You can no longer separate America and our culture of guns.

As our political and social climate changed in the last 50 years, average Americans began buying guns for purposes other than hunting or sporting. Gun sales also exploded in a way unseen in our past. Since over 80% of the guns available in the United States are manufactured here, gun production is a reasonable indicator of the guns made available. The following data is from a U.S. Department of Justice July 1995 report:

From 1973 to 1993, according to Bureau of Alcohol, Tobacco, and Firearms (ATF) data, U.S. manufacturers produced the following handguns alone:

6.6 million .357 Magnum revolvers
6.5 million .38 Special revolvers
5.4 million .22 caliber pistols
5.3 million .22 caliber revolvers
4.5 million .25 caliber pistols
3.1 million 9-millimeter pistols
2.4 million .380 caliber pistols
2.2 million .44 Magnum revolvers
1.7 million .45 caliber pistols
1.2 million .32 caliber revolvers

The ATF estimates that from 1899 to 1993 about 223 million guns became available in the United States, including over 79 million rifles, 77 million handguns, and 66 million shotguns. The number of guns seized, destroyed, lost, or not working is unknown. The number of new handguns added to those available has exceeded the number of new shotguns and rifles in recent years. More than half of the guns added in 1993 were handguns.

According to this FBI data, since the mid-1990s, the U.S. civilian gun inventory has increased from around 192 million total, with roughly 64 million handguns, to 265 million firearms, including 112 million handguns. By 2015, Americans overall owned more firearms and some people owned both handguns and long guns. Around 10 percent of owners had ten or more firearms, making up almost about 40 percent of all guns. Seventy million firearms changed hands between buyers from 2011 to 2015. Two and a half percent of Americans had guns stolen from 2010 to 2015, accounting for an estimated five hundred thousand guns getting into the hands of criminals.

This dynamic has changed dramatically since that last report. Handguns were the main topic as their sales exploded in America. It was easy to see that much of this was a result of citizens responding to fears, real or imagined, of being the victims of crime. In recent years, politics has become a driving factor. As people now arm themselves for civil strife, the move has been towards high-capacity military assault-style firearms. It is difficult to get accurate current data on this trend because so many sales have gone unreported through purchases at gun shows, private sales, and online purchases. Some data on this explosion of purchases exists only in part and is unfortunately anecdotal at best. The other problem with data in the last decade or so is that the FBI and ATF need more time to compile and analyze what has been happening with these off-the-books sales between individuals who are bypassing the existing rules for gun purchases.

The military has developed many hand-held firearms that can fire all types of exploding shells, some that can even stop a tank. These can be laser-guided or even be "wire-guided," in which a spool of wire shoots out with the projectile, allowing the shooter to modify where the projectile goes by moving the wire.

Other historical developments in firearms have included advances in ammunition. There are exploding or burning rounds that were developed for special purposes. Some firearms have burning bullets to show the shooter where the bullet is going during its flight. These bullets, called tracers, are used predominately by the military, but private citizens also use them.

I have personally seen another example of a special weapon while working as a police officer in Barrow, Alaska. Native hunters used bullets called "whale bombs" fired from a whale gun.

These date from the late 19th century, but Inuit Eskimos hunting Bowhead whales in the Arctic still use them today. The gun is heavy and made of brass, like an old-fashioned cannon. It is a shoulder-fired weapon. After harpooning a whale, hunters pull in the rope attached to the harpoon, and once they have pulled their walrus-skin boat is alongside the whale, they shoot the whale. The bullet, or bomb, goes into the whale, exploding a huge amount of black powder. Thousands of pieces of copper shrapnel from the bullet quickly go through and kill the whale, allowing the hunters to harvest it more humanely, and to reduce the danger to the Inuit hunters maneuvering in the freezing waters of the Arctic Ocean.

The last feature defining modern firearms is the design of the brass casing that holds the bullet and the gunpowder itself. New versions make bullets faster and more efficient than older ones. Shotguns that used to have shells of paper, which some still do, have been mostly replaced by plastic ones. There are also bullet cases that are now made of aluminum and steel instead of brass. Steel is commonly used in Russian and Chinese ammunition to save on costs. These new cases also contain bullets with new and improved ballistic performance, which we discuss in Chapter Seven, "How a Bullet Works."

.50 caliber weapons were once only for the military, but citizens can buy some of them today.

CHAPTER SIX

BASIC TYPES OF MODERN FIREARMS FOR SALE TODAY

The descendants of those ancient discoveries involving gunpower and firearms now come in three basic categories: Smooth-Bored Firearms, Rifled Firearms, and Shotguns.

Smooth-Bored Firearms

Other than shotguns, firearms without rifling in the barrel are called muskets, or sometimes just smoothbores. Old-fashioned "black powder" firearms had smooth bores and were nowhere nearly as accurate as later rifled weapons. Modern black powder firearms now have rifling in the barrel for accuracy, but like their historical antecedents, can only fire one shot at a time. They do not use a shell to hold the gunpowder and the bullet. Instead, gunpowder is poured down the barrel, followed first by wadding, and then the bullet, which is then tamped down with a ramrod. These weapons are slow to operate and are seldom used in criminal activity today. Think of someone in a raccoon skin hat with buckskin pants and shirt with fringes, like in the old movies, and you get the idea.

Flintlocks were smooth-bored firearms that used a piece of hard stone, flint, on a lever, that once you pulled the trigger, struck a piece of steel to set off a spark that ignited and fired the weapon. Flintlocks are mostly museum pieces today.

Black powder guns are primarily used for target shooting or for hunting in special limited seasons.

Rifled Handguns and Rifles

Rifled handguns and long rifles fire a bullet that travels down a barrel that has "rifling" or twisting grooves cut into the metal of the bore. The rifling makes the bullets spin and travel straight. Rifling works on the same principle as a gyroscope: Something spinning when traveling through the air does not change course without some other force acting on it.

Rifles vary from single-shot hunting rifles to those shooting 40 or more rounds in a clip in fully automatic military-style assault weapons. Similarly, handguns come in single-pull one-shot-at-a-time revolvers, to semi-automatic handguns that can also be made to fire fully automatically.

Long Gun. This term refers to the length of the barrel of a firearm but is also used generally to mean a rifle. There is little functional difference between a rifle and a rifled handgun, outside of the length of the barrel and the stock. A long and rifled weapon is more accurate than a shorter one. A carbine is just a firearm that is shorter than a standard rifle and longer than a handgun, shoulder-fired like a hunting rifle.

Double Action Handguns. Handguns fire a single round each time you pull the trigger. With a double-action handgun, you simply pull the trigger until the hammer comes all the way back and then falls, driving the firing pin into the bullet. You do not have to cock this gun to fire it because that happens automatically when you pull the trigger. These are the most common handguns today. Each time you fire, a new bullet is advanced into the firing position.

Single Action Handguns. Some older or cheaper pistols are "single-action" handguns. When you pull the trigger, nothing happens. First, you must pull the hammer back and lock it into place, cocking the gun. Then you can pull the trigger and fire the weapon.

Many older or historic handguns are of a single-action variety. It is amusing that in many western movies, the handguns are clearly single-action weapons (think of seeing the cowboy in a movie fanning the hammer with the trigger pulled) but they magically fire double action, and of course, usually fire many more rounds than any revolver could hold. This weapon also advances a new bullet into the firing position with each shot.

Revolvers. The action of a revolver includes a round cylinder containing five or six bullets. It turns after each shot, advancing the next bullet into the chamber in line with the firing mechanism and the barrel. You can fire all five or six bullets before having to re-load.

Derringers. There are some handguns that typically hold only one bullet, or sometimes have two barrels that each fire one bullet, in either case, with a single pull of the trigger. They are called "derringers," a common misspelling of their patented action by the Deringer company. They are notable for being very small and concealable. They can fire many different types of rounds of ammunition from very tiny to huge and powerful. In western movies, these are the pistols that you will see professional card players wearing on retracting mechanisms up their sleeves. When somebody accuses the gambler of cheating, he trips the concealing mechanism, the pistol drops into his hand, and he aims it around the card table as he scoops up the money and runs. These weapons are notoriously inaccurate beyond a few feet but can still be deadly: A Deringer was the pistol that John Wilkes Booth used to assassinate Abraham Lincoln. Women like derringers because they are light and concealable, but they are a terrible choice because they are so inaccurate beyond a foot or so and are easy to wrest from the owner.

Shotguns

Shotguns are smooth bored long firearms that usually fire pellets, not bullets. Shotguns can fire also a very large single projectile, called a slug, but more commonly, they fire multiple pellets available in varying sizes in a shell, or "load." The pellets inside the shell are contained in a plastic "wad" that keeps them together until they leave the barrel of the shotgun. That inside plastic wad opens when it hits the air, and the individual projectiles spread out as they travel forward, spreading further apart as they fly. The plastic usually drops harmlessly not far from the muzzle of the shotgun.

A slug fired from a shotgun can also be rifled to travel in more of a straight line, but because they travel much more slowly than a rifle bullet, they are not good at shooting for long distances. In shorter distances, they are very powerful and can shoot through a car or several walls or metal structures.

"Buckshot" is among the largest of the common multiple projectiles fired from a shotgun, and a standard 12-gauge shotgun's load of #00 Buck usually contains about nine large pellets. They can easily kill people and large animals. By contrast, bird hunters use shotguns with much smaller size pellets, but with many more pellets per casing.

The "gauge" of a shotgun refers to the diameter of the barrel and the type of shell it fires. The biggest is a 10 gauge, followed in descending order by the 12-, 20-, and 410-gauge shotguns. Gauge is determined by the number of lead balls of size equal to the approximate diameter of the bore that it takes to weigh one pound. For example, it would take 12 lead balls with the same diameter as a 12-gauge shotgun bore to weigh one pound.

Shotguns are classified, generally, into the categories of single or double-shot, pump-action, and automatic varieties, describing how they are cocked and fired. The single or double-shot variety often breaks (bends open) in the middle when a button is pressed, ejecting the last used-up round or shell. You then must insert the new round into the chamber and close it back up before firing. Sometimes this cocks the trigger and sometimes it must be cocked again before firing. Some have two triggers to fire either one or both barrels at once.

Other shotguns are loaded from the bottom or side. You can put several rounds or shells into the holding mechanism where they will wait until the gun is "racked" or reload the next one into the chamber to fire it. In the case of an automatic shotgun, reloading happens automatically each time a round of ammunition is fired.

For police work when I carried a shotgun, which I often did in highly dangerous situations, I always had some loads of #00 buckshot and a few slugs at the ready. For many tactical situations, this was often my ultimate weapon of choice. It can kill someone quickly.

People who are aficionados always love some certain gun. It's like their favorite sports team or favorite car brand that can do no wrong. Although I could generally fire a perfect or near-perfect score at any standard police firing range, I have never been a gun nut. I have always seen firearms as tools for hunting or work. If I suggest a gun or type of gun, it is based on my personal experience. I can promise you that for everything I say in this book, there is someone out there who loves guns who will disagree, vociferously, with my suggestions or comments. Don't let that bother you. Their experiences are not the same as mine. There is always an exception to every rule, and there are no perfect answers to choosing a firearm for any certain situation, but I know what I am talking about.

CHAPTER SEVEN

HOW A BULLET WORKS

Weapons today fire stable gunpowder that does not explode, even if you throw a match into it. It just burns. Most modern gunpowder can explode only if it is contained in a confined space.

The typical ignition source for modern firearms is a "primer," a stable chemical like mercury fulminate which is a contact explosive. The brass or silver-colored cartridge with the pointed lead bullet on the end is called the "shell" or "case" and it contains the gunpowder. When the trigger is pulled, the hammer of the gun strikes the primer with a firing pin, the primer explodes, igniting the gunpowder, which also explodes, propelling the bullet out the end of the barrel.

Basic Ballistics

Although it is easy to understand how a gun fires, very few people have a good understanding of how a bullet works after it leaves the barrel of a firearm and strikes its target. Most people think a bullet kills a person or an animal because it punches a hole in them. This is generally not true unless the bullet goes directly through the brain, heart, or lungs. Rather, a bullet kills with force, internal slicing through tissue and physical shock, not just shock from blood loss.

A modern bullet can leave the barrel of a rifle at around 3,000 feet per second. That's 2,045 miles per hour. Even sticking your finger in a glass of water at that speed would destroy your finger like it was hitting a brick wall. That's called the "shock factor." The longer the barrel, the more time the bullet has gain speed before leaving the muzzle. Generally, handgun rounds travel slower than rifle rounds because the barrel is shorter, but the larger caliber ones still go fast enough to do substantial damage.

You probably have seen a policeman on TV or in movies who was shot while wearing a bulletproof vest. He is luckily saved by this protective clothing. He looks at the bullet stuck in the vest with a sigh of relief. But that is not how it works in real life. When people are hit with a bullet, their skin and organs cannot absorb and dissipate the force, the sudden impact and energy of a bullet, quickly enough. On impact, before the bullet even enters, the entire area is subjected to immense damage. Sometimes this is fatal in and of itself. The shock can be so great with some ammunition that parts of a person's body can seem to vaporize. In slow motion, this looks like a mist that just dissipates into the air. Even with less impact, a bullet hitting a bulletproof vest hits the officer at such a high rate of speed that it knocks out his or her breath. The vest and outer clothing can be pushed deep into the chest, even though the bullet has not penetrated anything.

So many officers with "bulletproof" vests were being killed in the early days of their use that a metal "shock plate" was added to the front of the vest over the heart and lungs. That helped spread the force of a bullet over a larger area, making it less destructive.

Today many vests have ceramic shock plates that shatter with the first bullet strike. That absorbs the shock, like the crumple zones in a modern car. Many officers are saved by bulletproof vests, but they can still suffer very significant injuries because of the shock and energy of a bullet hitting them.

Some high-velocity bullets generating such great shock and force are no good for hunting. Animals shot with too high of velocity rounds will suffer so much damage as to be "blood-shot" and as much as a quarter of the animal is useless as food because it is destroyed by the energy of the bullet. Responsible hunters understand this and do not use such rounds.

Some rounds, like the Wetherbee .300 Magnum or .458 Winchester Magnum, were developed for killing elephants or other large African animals. Some hunters still use them for smaller North American game and most animals shot with them can be destroyed on impact due to this shock factor. This is wasteful and foolish.

Most non-military tactical bullets have lead tips, and some are open on the end. They are called "hollow-point" bullets. As soon as they hit something water-based, like an animal or a body, the relatively soft tip quickly flattens out and begins to "mushroom" and grow larger than the diameter of the original bullet diameter. As it flattens out on the end and opens, pieces also begin to shear off and spin into the surrounding tissue and organs. A single bullet at high speed can deposit hundreds of pieces of bullet shrapnel into the body. That is why some victims of gunshots have multiple surgeries to remove bullet "fragments." Some will have stray bullet parts in their bodies that show up on x-rays for the rest of their lives.

Hollowpoint bullets can deform more than solid bullets. Hollowpoints can also have small scoring on the copper jacket near the bullet tip. This causes the copper part of the bullet to open further and the expanding copper pieces, or "claws" rip through an even larger area just like a buzz saw. The damage from this type of bullet goes far beyond the area of the original diameter of the bullet. This expanding and fragmenting of the bullet is designed to hit as many veins and arteries as possible on the way in before stopping. Expansion and damage from the slicing copper pieces and energy shock is the intent. Most victims of a gunshot who die do so from the tissue damage in the surrounding area and the catastrophic bleeding that is associated with it.

Bullets that are not fully encased in metal jackets all way over the lead tips are sometimes called "dum-dums," although this term is not used much anymore. It was used extensively about the time of WWI and began to fall out of use in the 1960s, but is the language used in the Geneva Convention to describe a general category of bullets that expands.

Bluntnose, full metal jacket, slower, and cheap ammunition also have purposes. They are used for target practice and military use. They cost only a fraction of the cost of tactical rounds like the ones that police officers have in their duty weapons. Bullets designed for target practice do not work well to kill someone because of their low velocity, small size, and low kinetic energy, but a significant number of people use these bullets in their guns for self-defense because they do not understand the ballistics of bullets and the difference between the two uses.

To save cost, many of the inexpensive target rounds do not have copper jackets. They are just a lump of lead. The shells are thin and are often made of less expensive metals or sometimes even plastic. They have less powder and are designed only to shoot paper targets at a range and cannot contain the pressures of exploding high-velocity tactical rounds that are used for self-defense or police work.

Besides the damage caused by the shock and force of a bullet, there are secondary injuries from bullet wounds that can also have lasting impacts on a person who is shot. I was working early one morning in my police career when I was called to a shooting at a Radio Shack store. When we got there, a guy was lying on the ground. He and the store were a bloody mess, but he was alive. You would probably be surprised at how much some people bleed when they are shot. I was a detective at the time and was sent to the hospital with this victim to recover the bullets from his body to hold as evidence. We went to Harborview Hospital, a top-level trauma facility with some of the best surgeons in the world. I was invited in by the surgical team, put on a gown and mask, and stood by the guy's head so I was not in the way. This way doctors could just hand me the bullets and I would be able to see where they came from and testify about it. This could spare the surgeons' having to come to court later to testify at a trial, something they do not care to spend their time doing.

I happen to find surgery fascinating, but it is not for everyone to see in person. Emergency room surgical processes are not gentle. Time is everything when it comes to saving a person's life. The doctors quickly took a saw, like a skill saw that you might have at your home, and sawed his chest open in just a few moments. Then they stuck in huge clamps that pulled his chest wide open from the sides. His heart had been struck by one of the bullets that didn't go all the way through and into the chamber. They pulled his heart up from his chest cavity and stitched up the small tear on the side while it was still beating. They then reached into his chest cavity and pulled out a big hand full of coagulated blood. Even I had to admit that this was a little bit gross. After they took out the blood, they pulled out two bullets, one from his lung cavity and one that had lodged into his liver. The

.50 Cal. Bullet
.22 Cal. Bullet
.22 Cal. Short Cartridge
.357 Magnum Cartridge
.40 Cal. Smith & Wesson
9mm Cartridge
.270 Rifle Cartridge
Flat Nosed Bullet
Hollow Point Bullet

Typical bullets and cases - size comparison.

20-gauge

410-gauge

12-gauge

Metal Base

Plastic Shell

Primer

Gun Powder

Wad

Shot or Pellets

Inside a 12-gauge shotgun round with BB-sized pellets, and three different size shotgun shells.

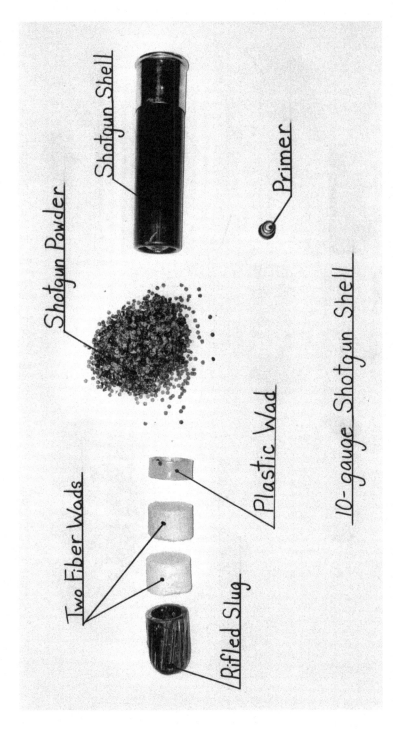

Shotgun Shell

Shotgun Powder

Primer

Plastic Wad

Two Fiber Wads

Rifled Slug

10-gauge Shotgun Shell

This 10-gauge shotgun round is the largest, and you can see the single large rifled slug that this one fires. It can shoot through a car or many walls.

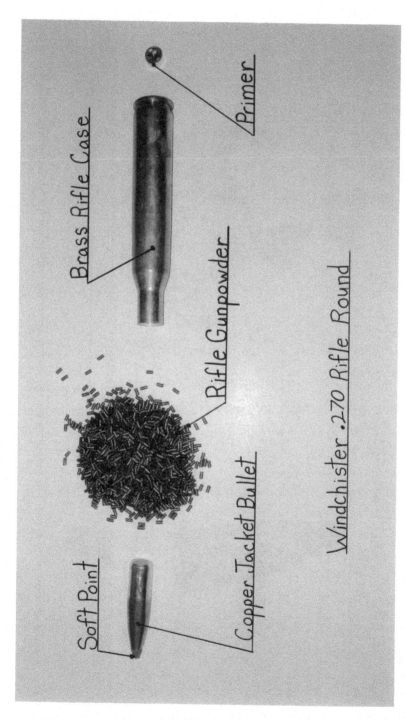

Primer

Brass Rifle Case

Rifle Gunpowder

Copper Jacket Bullet

Soft Point

Windchister .270 Rifle Round

Parts of a rifle or handgun round of ammunition.

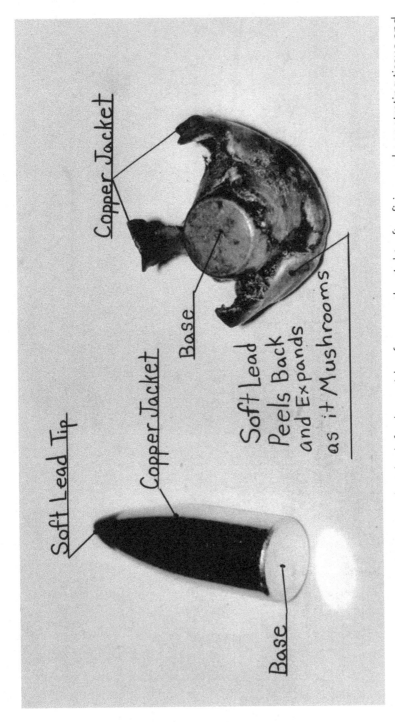

Soft Lead Tip

Copper Jacket

Base

Copper Jacket

Base

Soft Lead
Peels Back
and Expands
as it Mushrooms

A typical unfired non-military round to the left, along side of one on the right, after firing and penetrating tissue and bone with full expansion.

Comparison of shotgun projectiles sizes.

surgeons gave me the bullets and I stuck them into a paper evidence bag in some cloth so the blood on them would dry out and not rot.

These shots had been fired while the suspect and victim were fighting. They entered from the top of each of the victim's shoulders and went down through his chest cavity in a big X shape, crossing in about the middle of his chest. They were the result of a gun attack that had gone very wrong. The first shot had hit him in the leg (not at all unusual for a small automatic handgun which is notoriously inaccurate in the stress of combat) and then he had fought with the attacker hand-to-hand. The attacker finally delivered the second and third shots at point-blank range pointing down from the top of his shoulders while they were both on the ground wrestling. Any more powerful weapon or proper bullets would have killed him almost instantly.

The victim didn't die, but even though he lived, his mind was pretty much destroyed by the lack of oxygen for so long due to his excessive internal bleeding. When he woke up in the hospital, he asked me who I was. I told him I was Detective Hurst. Then he asked where he was. I said he was in the hospital. He asked why. I said he was shot. "I'm shot? Who are you?" And we would begin the same series of questions repeatedly. This 20-second loop is all his mind could contain and it never stopped being like that, first for weeks, then for months. We eventually figured out that his wife's ex-boyfriend attempted this murder to try to get her back.

The point here is that bullets can destroy a person's life, and the lives of those around them, in many ways. It also shows how a handgun can fire a bullet that does not do what bullets on TV or in the movies do.

The bad guy in this case simply got a "gun" and did not know much about it or the bullets it contained. To him, it was just a gun, like any other gun, and he thought it, and the bullets that were in it, would accomplish what he wanted. He planned to walk in, shoot the gun at the guy, hit him in the heart, see him fall dead on the floor and that would be the end of it. Then he would get his old girlfriend back. Instead, this first shot with his semi-automatic handgun hit the victim in the leg. When he finally made what might have been fatal shots, the bullets failed to do what he wanted them to because they were small, slow target rounds. This bad guy's knowledge of guns and bullets was average for most people in America today. This may surprise you, but it is true.

A Myth & Military Ammunition

Police bullets and military bullets are different and have vastly different purposes. Police and hunting bullets are designed to kill people or animals. By contrast, military bullets do sometimes kill but are designed more for wounding and not killing or injuring people as seriously as do nonmilitary and police bullets. There is a simple reason for this. Bullets like the ones that the police use and the ones used for killing a deer are illegal in military conflicts. They have been illegal since 1899 and their use is an international war crime today. Although people who love their military-style weapons and believe that they are the ultimate killing machines do not believe this, here is the actual language from the Geneva Conventions that makes them illegal:

> *The Contracting Parties agree to abstain from the use of bullets which expand or flatten easily in the human body, such as bullets with a hard envelope which does not entirely cover the core or is pierced with incisions." Declaration (IV,3) concerning Expanding Bullets. The Hague, 29 July 1899.*

According to Section 6(1)(b)(xix), "[e]mploying bullets which expand or flatten easily in the human body, such as bullets with a hard envelope which does not entirely cover the core or is pierced with incisions", constitutes a war crime in international armed conflicts.

Now, many will vehemently deny that this exists at all, and some will point out that America has not signed onto some of the more recent elements of the Geneva Conventions. The second point is valid, but the provisions about bullets from 1899 still apply and the U.S. did sign these. Moreover, look at how America treats expanding bullets in its established rules for armed service members in combat. Here are but a few examples:

United States of America

The US Military Field Manual (1956) states: "Usage, has ... established the illegality of ... the scoring of the surface or the filing off of the ends of the hard cases of bullets

United States of America

The US Air Force Pamphlet (1976) states: International law has condemned dum dum ... bullets because of types of injuries and inevitability of death. Usage and practice has also determined that it is per se illegal ... to use irregularly shaped bullets or to score the surface or to file off the end of the hard cases of the bullets which cause them to expand upon contact and thus aggravate the wound they cause.

United States of America

The US Instructor's Guide (1985) stresses the prohibition of "irregular-shaped bullets such as dum-dum bullets

The Guide also provides: "In addition to the grave breaches of the Geneva Conventions, the following acts are further examples of war crimes: using ... forbidden arms or ammunition such as dum-dum bullets.

You can see from these quotations that America's own military field manuals prohibit the use of dum-dums, which is just another term for expanding bullets. People will argue vociferously against the idea that military ammunition is not as deadly as is civilian and police ammunition. Online, you can see literally thousands of pages of posts calling this statement liberal nonsense, a myth. But it is their belief that is a myth. Let's look at the facts.

Military bullets are commonly called "full metal jacket" bullets. The inside is made of lead, or in some cases steel. The "jacket" is a copper cover that goes all the way from one end of the bullet to the other. It looks like a little copper missile all the way from the blunt end to the point. It is not made of soft lead on the tip. The tip is not flat. The tip does not have a hole in it. The copper shroud does not have any scoring along its side. Those features would make the bullet expand and spin off pieces into the person being shot and do far greater damage. Military bullets will not deform much upon entering the body. They remain the same size as they go through a body as opposed to growing three, four, or even five times larger as they travel through human tissue. Expanding bullets would do almost infinitely more damage and the military uses them only rarely, even then only in special circumstances.

Police do not want to use a firearm until it is necessary, but when they do, they mean for it to kill, and not merely wound a person. The military realized that wounding people requires soldiers to attend to a wounded comrade, thus tying up the fighting force in assisting people who need medical attention. This statement will also be attacked by advocates for military bullets. They do not understand the goal of most warfare. They think that wars are glorious events that are all about the macho killing of others. The actual goal of war is for one side to prevail, making one's opponents an ineffective fighting force until it surrenders, then to end the conflict as quickly as possible. If that objective can be achieved with fewer deaths in modern warfare, so much the better.

Bullet Performance & Uses

The old movies of police firing warning shots or shooting to wound, but not kill, are complete fiction. No police officer has ever had any such training. When necessary to shoot, police fire only to kill, aiming at what is called "center body mass" or the area that is in roughly the middle of a person's chest, where the heart and lungs are located. Hitting a person's lungs or heart will usually cause bleeding out internally, sometimes in a few seconds, and usually within a few minutes. Plummeting blood pressure will cause unconsciousness, and death follows. Just wounding does not neutralize a threat. Police do not aim for the shoulder, head, or stomach areas. A person's head is too small a target. Bullets that might land there are only by accident.

The ammunition used affects how well a handgun serves its police tactical or home defense purpose. The .357 magnum round for a revolver and the .40 caliber Smith & Wesson automatic round are excellent bullets for self-defense. They are large and powerful enough to stop someone. Some 9mm rounds are also okay, but they come in different sizes and smaller ones may not work well. Small caliber ammunition, like a .22 or small-caliber handgun rounds like a .25 or a .32, can, of course, be deadly, but often are not. Many shoot low-velocity bullets. A .22 pistol shoots a bullet at roughly

1,200 feet per second and the bullet is very light. These weapons are not good for self-defense because they can't reliably kill a person.

A close friend of mine, a fellow former law enforcement officer and colleague when we worked at the city of Tukwila, Washington, responded to an active shooter in a large shopping mall. He saw the bad guy with the gun and ran up to him to save others. The bad guy shot him seven times with a .22 caliber rifle before my friend took the gun away. Although some of the gunshot wounds gave him some difficulties for years, not one of them was fatal. None stopped him at the time, nor did they keep him from disarming the shooter.

Smaller handguns and rounds are simply foolish to have for self-defense because they will not stop a bad guy. And no, the Walther PPK that James Bond carries is not what you are looking for. A friend who owned one tried a PPK at a target range and complained of "hang fire." There was a significant delay between the time the trigger was pulled, and the bullet fired, while the shooter's aim drifted off target. She sold it and replaced it with a Smith and Wesson revolver.

Many small-caliber handguns that women buy and carry for self-defense are nowhere near adequate to stop an attacker. It is a mistake to rely on them because they can easily be taken away and used against the owner, even by someone who has already been shot at with it! Some will say that a woman can't shoot a .357 magnum revolver or a .40 caliber Smith & Wesson automatic handgun due to the recoil. I disagree, as this is more about proper training than the gun and bullet itself. I also think that it is better to either use the proper firearm and bullet or not use one at all.

A friend of mine recently told me the story of a woman from Alaska who goes running in bear country with a small .22 handgun. People always tell her that she cannot kill a grizzly bear with a .22, to which she responds, "Of course. I know that. If I am attacked by a bear, the bullet is for me!" This woman has a keen awareness of bullet performance. A small concealable handgun with small ammunition that won't kill a person with the first round or two certainly can't win in a gunfight. Or kill a bear.

Different firearms can fire a variety of different size bullets, projectiles, or shells. A .22 is a small caliber bullet; on the other end of the spectrum, one of the largest bullets is a .50 caliber. A .50 caliber can kill a person almost two miles away and have it be - and were used to shoot through the sides of Navy Destroyer ships in WWII to sink them. But even the best gun, without the proper ammunition and understanding of how it works and where to place the bullet, can render it useless in a tactical encounter.

One last note is on steel ammunition for rifles or handguns. It is inexpensive. It's also common for people with military assault-style weapons, especially fully automatic ones, to buy and use because they fire so many bullets so quickly and this ammunition is cheap. Normal bullets are made of lead and are covered with copper. Both are extremely soft and flexible metals. Unlike softer lead and copper bullets, steel bullets do not compress easily, and the steel of the bullet damages the steel of the gun barrel as it passes through. Steel bullets create what is called a "shot out" barrel, ruining accuracy. It is like driving a car in the rain with no tread left on the tires.

Much ammunition shot out of military assault-style weapons is steel bullets. I run into people in the woods all the time and tell them that they are shooting steel bullets and ruining their firearms. The majority do not believe me. I carry a magnet and show them that their bullets are magnetic steel. They are destroying their guns with cheap ammunition and don't even know it.

Understanding ballistics and knowing how to choose the right caliber of weapon and the proper ammunition is a necessary part of gun ownership.

CHAPTER EIGHT

HOW ACCURATE ARE GUNS?

A ny firearm can be deadly, some are more precise an instrument than others, but the key to accuracy is the operator. We will talk more about certain firearms and calibers for different uses, in Chapter 13, "Choosing Your Firearm," in more detail.

How accurate is any firearm? Like every question in this book, the answer is – "it depends." A gun is a machine, and like pretty much every other machine, there are good ones and bad ones. Some are worthless and no matter who is using them, they are not and will never be reliable or accurate. They have flawed designs, or they are manufactured poorly. On the other hand, there are well-made and reliable firearms that work perfectly and would be extremely accurate but haven't hit that proverbial "broad side of a barn door" because of operator error.

There are four basic concepts to consider when evaluating firearms: reliability, safety, capacity, and accuracy. Americans are told that everything is all about capacity. Bigger with more bullets always seems to be better, and why not? Isn't it better to have 30 or

40 bullets than six? Not if you can't hit anything with them, if the gun does not fire, or you do not know how to use it. Any gunfight against another person that is not over after the first or second bullet is one you are probably going to lose.

Do not think that more complex or faster firing guns are always the best. They often are not at all, and many of the faster, popular, or more complex guns are notoriously inaccurate and can be prone to malfunction. Many popular military assault-style firearms are primarily offensive weapons intended to spray bullets rather than to aim precisely, and are poor defensive weapons in most situations, like in your home for self-defense. These are commonly marketed to young men, untrained in their tactical use, who see them as an extension of their manhood. In fact, gun manufacturer Remington advertised these weapons with an ad campaign that said, "Get Your Man Card Back!" The Sandy Hook mass murderer used one of these weapons. You do not need to be very accurate with one of these types of weapons when there are a lot of people in a small, confined space.

Another example of unreliability is the .45 automatic handgun that the US Army issued to officers in WWII. People love these old weapons. There are lots of them around. I have found them to be almost worthless. I always tell people that you can throw them at someone and probably have about as good a result as trying to shoot anything with them, and that is if they fire at all. Some people will disagree with me, but this is not their book, and I am just telling you what I know from my own experience. At the range, I have not seen any weapon with such a high misfire rate, or that is as inaccurate as these old WWII era .45 automatic handguns.

On May 17, 2015, there was a shootout in Waco, Texas at the Twin Peaks Restaurant involving over 200 participants, most of them members of motorcycle gangs. Police later recovered 320 weapons from the crime scene, many of them automatic or military assault-style rifles, like AK-47s. The police responded, and they too had automatic military assault rifles. When the shootout was over, only nine persons were killed and 18 were wounded. One-hundred seventy-seven were arrested. One might think that outlaw motorcycle gang members with automatic weapons, engaged in an all-out gunfight lasting for quite a while, starting in a restaurant and spilling out onto its parking lot, might end up with most of the people being dead; but even people who carry guns regularly are not necessarily good at using them to shoot other people. In Chapter Twelve, we will discuss killing people.

On February 7, 2022, there was an intriguing headline in the *Seattle Times* announcing that there had been a gunfight on the streets of a neighborhood at 2:30 in the morning. Witnesses reported that many people were involved in the shootout. After the shootout, suspects were seen fleeing on foot and in vehicles. When the police arrived, they found bullets all around the neighborhood. Bullets had hit houses, businesses, and cars. Police recovered dozens of bullet cases from the scene, not including any fired from inside the vehicles that had fled the area. What police did not find was any indication that anyone had been shot. Why? Once again, because of the operators.

In the third example of accuracy, I was on duty one day when a call came in reporting a shooting in progress. I was the first officer to arrive at the scene but missed the bad guys by about a minute. Other officers arrived and we got reports of events related to this crime scene showing up in other locations. A vehicle crashed into the side of the road a few miles away. The car hit an embankment, seriously injuring two young men. The driver did more than miss a turn—he was bleeding from a gunshot wound and lost consciousness. Besides being injured in the crash, the passenger had his spine severed near his hips by a bullet from a .308 hunting rifle that passed through him and into the driver.

You will have to excuse me, but the crime scene at the victim's home amused me. Bullet casings lay everywhere - - in the house, on the porch, in the driveway, in the yard. It looked like the shootout at the OK Corral. But no bodies were anywhere to be seen, nor even a drop of blood. The incident started as a purchase of $170 worth of marijuana. However, the bad guys didn't have $170. What they did have were guns. So of course, it made sense to them to pull out their guns and rob the seller. What could go wrong? The marijuana-buying bad guys had a Mac-10, which resembles a small hand-held submachine gun that you might see in a James Bond movie, plus an 9mm automatic handgun with extra clips of ammunition, just in case.

The drugs were displayed, the guns came out - - all within 10 feet of one another - - but unfortunately for the "buyers," the seller also had a 9mm automatic handgun with several clips of ammunition, because you just never know what to expect with drug customers. He pulled out his gun and the bullets began to fly. They shot at each other throughout the house with semi-automatic firearms. The gunfight spilled out onto the porch. They shot at each other in the yard and the driveway, reloading and leaving shell casings as the robbers fled to their vehicle.

The buyers realized they were never going to get the marijuana. They got to their vehicle just as the seller ran out of bullets for his handgun. He ran back into the house and retrieved a single-shot bolt-action .308 hunting rifle. As the buyers tried to drive away from the house, the seller shot a single bullet into the vehicle. It pierced the passenger door, severed the spine of the passenger, and stuck the driver.

The seller was never charged for the attempted drug sale, nor was he charged for shooting the buyers. The prosecutor deemed it a case of self-defense, although chasing after the fleeing would-be robbers might have well exceeded any right of self-defense. The buyers, including the paraplegic who is now in a wheelchair for the rest of his life, are both serving most of the rest of their lives in prison due to this incident and their extensive criminal histories.

This incident demonstrates two important points. First, bringing or displaying a gun in most situations is a terrible idea. Second, guns, especially automatic weapons in the wrong hands, are almost hopelessly inaccurate. Most people with automatic weapons will begin firing wildly because they have so many bullets to use up. They rely on the concept of having all these extra bullets to compensate for bad bullet placement and poor tactical techniques.

There is also a mental state that makes some people tactically incompetent, no matter how many bullets they have or how quickly their gun can fire. The faster they fire, the worse their shooting gets. This is, in part, because most Americans with firearms have no training, knowledge, preparation, or ability to bring to a gunfight.

Owning a gun and shooting at a range or in the forest does little to prepare a person for using firearms tactically. Many people with firearms in America are not capable of ever learning tactical skills.

Imagine a gunfight with just one person as your opponent, no matter how that person is armed. With any decently made firearm, the measure of accuracy in an armed conflict is determined by the intelligence, discipline, and training for such a situation, and even then, shooting to kill will be difficult. The gunfight should be over after the first shot or two. After that, it becomes the OK Corral, and then it's just up to luck.

SHOOTING LIBERALLY

Guns are not inherently accurate or inaccurate in and of themselves. Competence, preparation, intelligence, and courage are human traits.

Cash, drugs, and firearms are what people are looking for in most home invasion robberies. Pictured here is $438,000 in cash, cocaine and an automatic assault-style weapon.

CHAPTER NINE

HOME INVASION ROBBERIES

It's time to cover probably the scariest firearm encounter that most people in America fear today:

HOME INVASION ROBBERIES!

They are scary. Every time one happens, it makes front-page news. Right-wing media outlets tell you they happen all the time. They want to terrify you. They detail the horror of someone breaking in, tying you up, you and your family being tortured, raped, robbed, and killed. This is what these media outlets and some far-right politicians want you to think about, because it keeps viewers glued to their stations. Besides attracting advertising revenue, this fearmongering delivers donations to their favorite political candidates, and votes to the right-wing politicians.

To clarify, a "burglary" is an entry and theft done in secret in a residence or certain buildings, and these are common. A "robbery" is a person-to-person confrontation. Done in private residences, robberies are uncommon. Many home burglaries (or even home robberies) could have been prevented by a good home security system that deters, detects, and scares criminals away.

In a high percentage of home invasion robberies, the victim knows the intruder and the invaders are there for a known reason or relationship. Let me explain:

I once arrested a man named Troy Marlowe for drug trafficking. He agreed, as many people do, to cooperate as a witness against his higher-level suppliers. Our objective was always to get as far up the chain of distribution as possible and to file cases against those who run criminal enterprises, not just the lower-level workers. During his cooperation, I became aware of claims from others that Marlowe also ran a side business doing armed home invasion robberies.

I asked him about this, and he told me he had a very lucrative business. He knew his victims would never testify against him because they were criminals themselves. He told me in detail about how he and his crew, dressed in all-black outfits with face coverings like Ninja warriors, moved quickly, broke into houses, drew guns, and tied everyone up at gunpoint. He robbed them of cash and drugs. Competitors in the drug business do that to each other all the time.

Why would someone engage in this type of crime against you? It can get criminals many decades in prison, and most criminals know this. What would justify such a risk? Do you keep tens or hundreds of thousands of dollars of cash or cocaine in your house? A vast majority of these types of robberies are against known targets and are not random at all. The average non-criminal person is unlikely to become a victim of one.

When home invasion robberies are done by professional groups, homeowners will almost never be able to use their guns to stop it. They happen too fast. Criminals doing home invasion robberies do not slowly creep into a home. In a typical home invasion robbery, the criminals know their target is home. They intend to confront and compel the homeowner to tell where their illegal money and drugs are hidden. You can expect that a group doing home invasion robberies will have everyone at gunpoint within a second or two.

Unless you are wearing a gun on your person and are immediately ready to draw and use it within a second or two, having a gun in the general area will not work in a robbery. Trying to stop an event like this by trying to find and arm yourself with a firearm will increase the risk of your getting shot and killed.

In over 25 years of police work, I was called to only a small number of home invasions robberies at non-criminal households. In every case I investigated, the bad guys mistakenly hit the wrong house. They got out of the home as quickly as they could upon realizing there were no drugs or cash to steal. If the owners had tried to arm themselves, it is likely that the homeowner would be shot and killed.

There may be reasons to consider getting a gun or arming yourself to protect your home or family but defending against the risk of a home invasion robbery is not a good one.

CHAPTER TEN

SELF-ASSESSMENT - TAKE A SEAT ON THE COUCH

This may be the most important chapter in the book. How do you determine if you are an appropriate consumer to possess a gun, or have one in your home for self-defense? Doing a proper self-risk assessment is a critical part of gun ownership. I wish a great many more Americans would ask that question before buying one. Because you live in America, this assessment is left up to you. Citizens in other countries have guns, but they get some help in this assessment. That is why other countries experience fewer problems per capita involving guns than do Americans. Let's look at how this assessment works around the world, then you can see how you might want to proceed.

Most countries require an in-depth psychological assessment before allowing possession of firearms. America does not. At most, some state laws prohibit licensing concealed weapons for people with histories of certain types of disqualifying mental illness that could lead to self-harm or harm to others.

There is a great story about buying guns in 16 other nations, by Audrey Carlsen and Sahil Chinoy, in the New York Times from March 2, 2018, and August 6, 2019, "How to Buy a Gun in Sixteen Countries." Google this title and date and it should be easy to find. According to this review, the easiest country in which to get a gun was Yemen, where a firearm could be purchased online. That's it. In America, it is just a tiny bit more difficult. You need to pass an instant background check for criminal convictions, domestic violence, and immigration status, and wait for a three-day cooling-off period, at least when buying from a licensed dealer. Notoriously, "Gun Shows" have been lax in allowing anyone to walk in, buy a gun, and walk out with it, and private person-to-person sales aren't covered by laws at all.

By contrast, in Japan, New Zealand, South Africa, Mexico, Australia, Austria, Canada, India, Germany, Britain, Brazil, Russia, Israel, and China you must show that you are mentally stable enough to possess a gun. The test happens in various ways in different countries, but the idea is the same. A purchaser must be interviewed or pass a background check. Sometimes other people are interviewed about the buyer. Many people do not know that they are mentally unstable, but their family and friends sure do!

Most countries also require the safe storage of firearms. Purchasers need a storage plan, and often, an inspection of the storage plan is required in advance of the purchase.

Virtually all require a gun safety course. Purchasers must have at least some basic ideas on how to use, fire, practice with, or otherwise use a firearm before accidentally hurting or killing themselves or someone else. Brazil tests competence even further, requiring that the purchaser demonstrate hitting a target from 16 to 23 feet away at least 60 percent of the time. With a handgun, this is more difficult than a buyer might think, and a lot harder than it looks in a James Bond 007 movie.

Some countries ask why you want to buy a gun and what you plan to do with it. (Some potential buyers admit that they want a gun to kill a specific person. See the story of Wendy Wein who tried to hire a hitman to kill her husband: .https://www.washingtonpost.com/nation/2021/11/22/rent-a-hitman-website/ accessed 11 February 2022.)

Some people should never be allowed to buy a gun. Are you one of them? It is time to be honest. Test yourself in a few simple ways. First, do you use prescribed or OTC medications for mental or psychological issues of any type? Do the medications you take for any reason cause sleepiness, forgetfulness, or mood changes? Include anti-anxiety or anti-depressant medications and any other mood-altering drugs. Some medications have specific warnings for side effects as specific as "Homicidal Rages." There is no shame here, but it means you need to have a discussion with your doctor or a qualified professional. If your doctor advises against it, reconsider getting a firearm. Your professional advisor might ask you to make some modifications to your plan to keep you, and those around you safe. That may be easy to do. You might at least ask them if they have any reason to think you are a poor candidate to own a firearm.

The second question is: What do your family and friends think of your owning a firearm? If you are too unstable, they likely know this. You should carefully listen to them with an open mind. These discussions are an important part of the process of self-assessment before owning a firearm. We are not talking about mental illness here; we are talking about personality. Many people are clinically healthy but possess traits that are not compatible with safely owing a firearm, for instance, forgetfulness, clumsiness, or short temper. Your friends and family may love you but see these things clearly when you may not see them at all.

Bringing a firearm into a home for self-defense impacts everyone in the household. It should be a collective decision that every teenager and adult in the household understands. This will also facilitate making a proper safe storage plan. Other family members or housemates need to know what their responsibilities are when a firearm is present. They must know and follow the rules.

Your self-assessment should be ongoing. Mental states can change, as can relationships. If depression sets in, that's a reason to secure a weapon more carefully. Loss of a loved one, loss of a job, or loss of money can trigger major changes in a person's mental state. A relationship that is showing signs of deterioration, where behavior becomes controlling, is another red flag. Keep an open mind to these types of changes in yourself or others.

America's suicide rate explains why prospective gun owners need to do a psychological assessment on their own before considering gun ownership. If a man has a gun in the house, he is eight times more likely to commit suicide, according to a Stanford study published in June of 2020. A Harvard study in 2010 indicated that of 38,664 suicides in America, 19,392 were suicides by firearm. The number of others killed by a firearm in the same period was 11,078. That is almost twice as many people killing themselves intentionally using a gun in their homes, as compared to people who are shot otherwise. If a person attempts self-harm with a firearm, he or she will be successful 85% of the time. With drugs, that rate is only 3%.

Suicide is impactful, not just to persons who kill themselves, but to their families, friends, neighbors, and aid workers. You may not like what I am about to tell you now, but you need to understand it. Suicides are not like TV, movies, or video games. They are unfathomably gruesome. Most close-range firearm suicides result in a large part of the head being blown off. Sometimes just the bottom jaw is left, with the upper skull and brains blown apart into a mist that covers everything in the room. It is a mess. It looks like the walls were painted in blood, brains, and tiny pieces of skull. This is always the result when a high-powered rifle or shotgun is used.

When people use firearms to kill themselves, someone else will have to discover and clean up the mess. This happens 55 times every single day in America, 365 days a year, especially on holidays like Thanksgiving and Christmas.

The length of a rifle or shotgun makes it harder to use for suicide. Handguns are much more dangerous in these cases. People killing themselves with a rifle or shotgun must place it up under their jaw or in their mouths, then use their toes to fire it. It is not easy to do. Handguns can make direct contact with the head or chest to shoot it easily. All firearms must be kept in a way to minimize risks of suicide, but the risk is far greater with a handgun.

Many states now have laws called Extreme Risk Protection Orders for removing firearms from a person who is a threat to himself or others, even if they have not yet committed a crime. Don't wait for that. In a recent case, parents observed that their son, a young adult, had become reclusive, had begun dressing all in black like a Ninja, and had begun ordering guns and military paraphernalia through the internet. When they found his plans to kill a local realtor, they called the police, who were able to take his guns before he hurt somebody. Fortunately, they were proactive and safe.

Many drunks or alcoholics either do not know or do not admit that they have this condition. Alcoholism is a major reason not to get a firearm. Alcohol and firearms cannot be mixed.

When I was a detective on a specialized team some years ago, we were all very close and liked to have a drink some evenings after work. When we did, we all locked up our weapons in a secure area and double-checked for guns before someone had as much as a sip of beer. If you cannot accept this concept as an absolute requirement, or if you have a drinker in your house who might have access to the firearm when intoxicated, you should never buy, own, or allow a firearm in your house.

The next risk factor around having a firearm in the house is relationships. If you have ever struck another person in your household or broken any of that person's property in anger, then you should not have a gun. If a person in your household has struck you or broken your property, you should not allow a gun to be present in your household if that person ever has access to it. Statistically speaking, people who strike or break the property of others in domestic situations will often be willing to use a gun if one is available, especially if drunk and angry.

Even in America where our gun laws are lax, domestic violence can disqualify a person from gun ownership; however, often domestic violence gets discovered only if a person is convicted.

Asking these questions is part of your self-assessment of whether you should have a gun in your house. Your self-assessment needs to be brutally honest and forthright. You don't need to tell anyone, or overly dwell on the past, but you must face the realities of the impacts of not considering these matters before buying a gun. Lay these things on the table and give them careful consideration.

Further, assuming your household is safe, do you also have a plan, the time, money, and facilities to learn how to properly possess and use a firearm for home self-defense? At the moment, .357 ammunition for a S&W Model 66 costs around $.70 to a little over $1.00 per round of ammunition. An average training session will use roughly 250 rounds, costing up to $250, to get much of anything done on a training course. You will need dozens of these sessions to attain a high level of proficiency. Ongoing training will cost hundreds more. Allow four to five times as much training if you plan to use an automatic weapon. Eventually, ammunition will cost more than the gun itself. Tactical ammunition will cost far more than these training target rounds. But if you cannot commit to adequate training, you will be useless with the gun in home defense.

Where are you going to get experience? Unless you live in rural Montana or Alaska, you probably can't just walk out the back door and set up a shooting range. There are many commercial ranges in most parts of the country, both indoors and outdoors, and many have excellent instructors who can help you get started.

Target shooting ranges are a smart place to get training if they can prove to you that they mitigate the dangers of lead at their shooting ranges. Handling bullets, especially expended cases and slugs, exposes you to absorption of lead through the skin, and it is toxic. Good ranges always will be happy to discuss this with you.

Many ranges will not allow military assault-style semi-automatic weapons on their premises. Very few allow fully automatic weapons to be fired.

Can you shoot on public land? In some cases, the answer is yes, but there are many restrictions you need to understand and follow as part of your planning. If planning on using your firearm on any public lands, always check out the applicable laws in advance. Read Chapter Nineteen, "Firing Wild."

A final question for your self-assessment is whether you are dedicated enough to follow through. You can be lazy about many activities in your life, but not this one. If you get bored and taper off on projects, then a firearm is not for you. You must treat a firearm as being completely deadly 100% of the time, 24 hours a day, 365 days a year. Having one for general home defense is an endeavor that requires a commitment to make and follow through.

Guns in the hands of responsible owners might make them, their homes, and their other family members safer, but only if done properly.

CHAPTER ELEVEN

HOME DEFENSE ALTERNATIVES

There are many options for home defense, ranging from cheap to expensive, that may serve your needs better than procuring a firearm. Outdoors, you can install a camera system that lets you see who is approaching your house. You can install lights that are activated by motion at night. You can assure that you have decent locks on your house doors. You might have to do some remodeling to change windows that could be broken out to allow somebody to reach inside and grab a door lock. A stick placed in the track of a sliding door prevents anybody from sliding the door open. The list goes on, well beyond the scope of this book. Below, we discuss some alternatives to keeping a gun in your house.

Part 1 of 6 - Do Not Mind Your Manners

This is a precaution especially for women, who are particularly trained to be nice, courteous, gracious, and kind. Do not open your door for strangers who knock, or even for obnoxious callers whom you don't want to see. Be rude, shout to them through the door to find out who they are and what they want. (A friend had her drunken neighbor demand that she come outside one night to buy his motorcycle—as though a 75-year-old woman would want to take up motorcycle riding at night.) Beware of strangers who claim they need help and want to borrow your bathroom or telephone. They are just as dangerous as those people standing next to the highway waving their hands frantically to stop you, claiming they have kids in the car and need $20.00 for gas, or just two dollars more for gas. On the highway, call the State Patrol for them (or call the cops down on them.) At home, use your meanest voice. Tell them to fuck off.

Part 2 of 6 - Baseball

If your objective is to obtain a gun to defend yourself in your home, you may have missed an alternative so common that you may never have thought of it. It is something your kids or you probably used at some time in your life. It's a baseball bat. I know, it's not sexy like a brand-new automatic military-style assault AR -15 with 30-round clips, but guess what? It often can beat a gun in close combat. If your intruder is not armed, an aluminum or wood baseball will beat them every time.

Baseball bats are cheap, super available, and pose little to no risk if you store a couple of them in your home. Keep one by the door and one by the couch where you watch TV. No one will even pay much attention. It just looks like you didn't clean up your house very well. (I once found a claw hammer between the cushions of a couch in a friend's house.)

There is one other huge benefit of a baseball bat over a handgun. Unlike a firearm, it is, quite literally, the worst tool in your house to use to kill yourself.

Part 3 of 6 - Grizzly Bears

Not interested in the concept of hitting someone with a baseball bat? Another product that can be very effective at stopping an intruder, even one with a gun, is bear spray. It is highly effective at stopping a charging grizzly bear. It is not just the small self-protection personal spray the size of a lipstick that you may have seen, but the larger product that hikers carry when large bears are present, like on Glacier National Park back-country hikes.

One of the most popular brands is called Counter Assault, which comes in 10-ounce spray cans and can reach 40 feet to stop a Grizzly. Your bedroom is perhaps 20' across. This product can be purchased for around $60. It comes in a pouch that you can wear on your belt when hiking in bear country or fits on your bedside table. The website for Counter Assault claims that it will stop charging Grizzly bears 92% of the time. I can tell you from personal experience with this product that its effects will be much stronger on people than on bears. This may stop a person without using deadly force.

There are several benefits to having a spray in your home for self-defense. You are within range to use it anywhere in a common-sized house. You do not need to be very accurate. Anything in front of you will be inundated. Within a second, an invader will likely be on his knees, screaming and convulsing violently, or trying to leave the area.

The spray continues for eight seconds. You can give multiple short doses, or just empty the can all at once. Strong effects last 15 to 45 minutes. Milder effects last about two hours. If you do not get it in your eyes or breathe it in yourself, you have more than enough time to call the police, tie up your assailant with restraints, or just run away.

You could restrain an intruder with handcuffs, but not with personal or fantasy ones like people have for other reasons. They are not the right product because they can easily break or be opened. If you want handcuffs, always make sure they are of good quality, like the ones like the police use, and learn to use them properly.

Although I cannot say for sure, I suspect that it would be extremely difficult to commit suicide with this product, should anybody want to try. If bad guys steal it in a burglary, they will probably just use it on their friends when they are drunk at a party just to see what it does. It will never be seen as a cool weapon.

That all being said, this product is not entirely non-lethal. Although extremely rare, there have been deaths from its use. This usually happens when people have restricted breathing from the products or pre-existing medical conditions. It is not a product to be used without necessity, but in my opinion, a person entering your home and attacking you more than justifies its use.

Once deployed, pepper spray will linger and can quickly affect you as well as the intruder. You will need to leave and wait for the police outdoors unless you also access a gas mask. Protesters use them all the time, and you can find them for sale on the internet.

I would also check with all local, state, and federal laws, depending on where you live, before having or using bear spray. This product is considered a firearm in Canada and is not legal without the same permitting process as a gun. Never take or keep it someplace where it might not be legal or where weapons are not permitted, like courthouses or airports.

Some social media sites have recommended that women use wasp spray for home defense. I have no experience with this product, except on insects, so I cannot say whether that would work.

Obviously, bear spray has to be kept out of the reach of children.

Part 4 of 6 – Electrical Solutions

Another option to consider for self-defense is an electrical device to disable an attacker. You might be familiar with the product called a "Taser" that many police carry.

I must tell you that I have a bit of a personal bias regarding electricity—it frightens me. When I was a 2-year-old, I was sitting on a concrete floor and stuck a pin into a wall socket. It is about the only memory of my early childhood that I can clearly recall, but I can still see it as if it were just a moment ago.

Then, a few years ago, I was hiking in the mountains when heavy rain and a terrible thunderstorm overcame me. A shaft of lightning hit 10 feet in front of me. The lightning knocked me back and shocked the heck out of me. That only reinforced my misgivings about electricity. It's very painful. I'm quite sensitive to being confronted by electricity.

A Taser will work well in stopping most people, at least for a few moments, or even a minute, but just until you get them under control, or you can run away. A Taser fires two darts that stick into the target's body. They are like small hypodermic needles with hooks on the ends. They are attached to long electrical wires that carry the charge into the body. The charge is both painful and, in most people, temporarily disabling. Although a person will recover from the shock quickly, nobody will want it to happen again.

There are other electrical defense devices as well. Some work on contact. A few are designed for use on people, and some are specifically designed to use on cattle. You have likely heard of a "cattle prod." It is just a very powerful direct-contact cow Taser. Some devices have two electrodes separated by a couple of inches. When you push a button, a large arc of electricity jumps across these electrodes and makes a terrible electrical crackling sound that is frightening. As a person who stuck a pin in a wall socket and got hit by lightning, it has a really big impact on me!

Prods for use on people are called "stun guns" and are widely available on the internet for between $10 and $400. If you click one on, they look terrifying, and many people are scared away. That may be their best use, although I am not recommending it. If it fails in a tactical situation, I can pretty much guarantee that a bad guy will use it on you, even if just for the fun of seeing what it does to a person. Again, I oppose displaying weapons that you are not willing, able, and trained to use.

Police officers trained with and carrying Tasers are required to have been shocked by one. There is a good reason for this. They need to know what it does. If you carry a stun gun you should consider the same thing, but you will not like it.

Part 5 of 6 - Physical Training & Home Defense

Many people take physical self-defense or martial arts courses taught by professionals. Some of these are excellent, and they have the added benefit of getting students into shape. You would be surprised at how some physical training and a self-defense course can help you protect yourself if you are ever attacked or threatened by someone. Most bad guys try to prey on defenseless people who do not fight back. Even some simple skills and voice commands can empower you to make an attacking person quickly retreat. These types of courses are easy to find anywhere in the United States. They can also be a healthy and fun place to meet other people with similar objectives. People who have some skills that they have practiced have more confidence if faced with a threat. An attacker will sense this quickly and often just move on while you call the police or retreat yourself.

Part 6 of 6 - Never Bring a Gun to a Knife Fight

I like movies. Movies are a universal language that illuminates ideas and concepts that we can all relate to. Of course, movies are also mostly nonsense. But we enjoy the suspension of disbelief for two hours. People know they can't put on a mask and a cape and then fly; however, they'll rely on movies to get most of their beliefs about guns. You have probably seen a movie where a bad guy pulls out a knife or sword and does some fancy hand movements when facing the good guy. The good guy then pulls out a handgun and shoots from probably 100 feet away. The bad guy with the knife or sword falls dead on the ground with a single shot. The people in the scene and in the movie theater are impressed, and the audience howls with laughter. It works great for Paul Neuman and Harrison Ford every time. It makes sense, right? Not so much.

In truth, if two people are at least 20 feet apart, where one determined person has a knife and the other has a handgun, the person with the knife will win the encounter roughly nine times out of ten against most people with a handgun. "Win" is an interesting term here as it means that the person with the knife will inflict a fatal wound before being shot or injured by the person with the handgun, and that is if they were even shot at all. A knife is often a better weapon than a handgun at around 20 feet away or less. There are multiple reasons for this, and I will address a few of them in this chapter and some later in Chapter 12, "Killing People."

Most police shootings occur within six feet of their target. Not even police can shoot and hit people with a handgun from more than 50 feet away very often. Civilians will find it even more difficult than officers do, for three reasons. First, handguns are not highly accurate beyond 10 to 20 feet. It takes time to aim a gun, hold it steady, slowly exhale, squeeze the trigger carefully, and hit much of anything beyond a short distance. A quick draw, as you have seen in hundreds of movies, would almost never hit a target 50 feet away, absent hundreds of hours of practice. Second, the knife will win the fight because if you are attacked and are not properly trained, massive amounts of adrenaline will course through your veins, causing your heart to pound so hard you can hardly see straight. You can't aim well in that condition. Don't count on your handgun being very effective beyond six feet most of the time.

Third, another problem with shooting in a knife attack is that most of the guns people buy for protection, especially women, have very short barrels so they are concealable or lightweight. The shorter the barrel of the gun, the less accurate it will be. You aim a gun by lining up the front sight with the rear sight while pointing it at the middle of your target. A gun finds its accuracy based on the distance between the rear and front sight. Shorten that distance and you can't hit much beyond six feet in an actual gunfight. In the meantime, the bad guy can cross the room and grab your weapon and stab you.

James Bond may carry a Walther PPK with its short barrel, but given a sock with a rock in it, you might beat 007 in an armed encounter and never get shot. These very short, small-caliber handguns are notoriously inaccurate and seriously underpowered.

One of my favorite movie scenes is from the Mel Brooks comedy, Blazing Saddles, where a Gene Wilder character, the Waco Kid, shoots and hits some dynamite from about three miles away with his handgun, blowing up the town. This is obviously a joke for the audience to laugh at, but most movies are not comedies like this one. They make these types of shots or unrealistic firearm performance seem real.

Wyatt Earp, a real lawman of the old west, carried a .45 caliber revolver called a "Peacemaker" with a 12-inch barrel. That is because he understood weapons, and with that length, it would be accurate at greater distances.

A sheriff's deputy I once worked with earlier in my career, Detective Michael Raburn, went to serve a court order in Seattle on March 27, 1984. The resident at the location opened the door and stabbed Detective Raburn in the chest with a WWII sword. As he fell back, Detective Raburn fired off several shots while retreating, but he died not long after. What is accurate about a knife as opposed to a gun encounter is even truer when a sword is involved. A sword, especially in the hands of a person with some training, is almost infinitely more dangerous than a firearm.

I have seen people who, after being hit numerous times by bullets, were still returning fire. A book called *Street Survival - Tactics for Armed Encounters,* by Special Agent Ronald J. Adams and Lieutenant Thomas M. McTernan and Charles Remsberg, popular in the 1980s, has an example of a police firefight where a man who was hit 33 times by police firing 9mm handguns, was still shooting back. No such thing happens when a major injury is inflicted with a sword.

I am not suggesting that police carry samurai swords, but for home defense, you should know that a long sharp kitchen knife in the hands of the right person is a more dangerous weapon than a gun at very close ranges.

A significant number of all police officers who were shot and killed in the line of duty (as opposed to suicides) over the years were killed with their own service weapons. In Washington State some years ago, three consecutive police officers killed in the line of duty were killed with their own handguns. Although most officers fire their weapons within six feet, using a handgun at such close range poses the problem of someone taking the gun away. Try grabbing a sword, or even a 12-inch kitchen knife out of someone's hand. It's virtually impossible to do without getting a serious or fatal injury.

"Little Cowboy" and his partner tried to kill my partner with a pearl handeled .45 automatic during a bust. It was a close combat handgun fight with no shots fired.

Once I was serving a narcotics search warrant in the Seattle area. The suspect in the case was a bad guy whom I had sent to prison twice in the previous decade. He opened his front door after we announced that we had a warrant. Out came his hand with a gun. It was a close call, but I grabbed the gun before he could fire it at me. My finger ended up behind the hammer and I pushed the barrel of the gun up into the air as I squashed the door against him to crush his arm. I was able to get him to let go of the gun, and after a short scuffle, he was arrested. If he had been armed with a sword, I would have likely been killed at such a close range.

A sharp weapon can go through many ballistic vests. Ballistic vests are layers of fiber designed to absorb the shock and impact from spinning bullets, not sharp cutting-edged weapons. Even highly trained police officers wearing vests can get stabbed.

At closer ranges, within six feet, keeping control of one's firearm gets more difficult. One night, I was assigned to a federal narcotics task force, and my partner was doing an undercover buy of a large amount of cocaine from a member of the Sinaloa Cowboys, an extremely violent Mexican organized crime family. We recognized them well from a distance because many of them carried pearl-handled .45 automatic handguns, had Brahma bull stickers on their truck windows, and lariats on their rearview mirrors. They also wore gold necklaces depicting the patron saint of drug traffickers, Jesus Malverde (not recognized by the Catholic Church I might add). We thought it was a cool "uniform" for an organized crime family, but we remembered that they were also exceptionally violent and thought nothing of killing others.

As the bust was going down, my partner Frank was wearing a wire so we could hear what was going on, but only one of us on the bust team spoke Spanish. Frank was fluent, and he was talking in Spanish with a bad guy who was known on the street as, "Little Cowboy." But with the language issue, there was some confusion with the bust signal and things began to go wrong.

Little Cowboy pulled out his .45 automatic and tried to shoot Frank in the abdomen as they were sitting side by side in the cab of the truck. Frank grabbed the gun and pushed Little Cowboy's hand up, so the gun was pointed to the top of the truck. Frank pulled out his own handgun and tried to shoot Little Cowboy in the mid-section near his heart and lungs – either of which would quickly be fatal. Little Cowboy grabbed Frank's gun and pushed it up too, and as their struggle went on, our team arrived and jerked open the door. By then, Frank had used the butt of his gun to pound a significant dent in Little Cowboy's head. When we opened the door, both men fell out and dropped their guns in the dark on the side of the road and continued wrestling. A second bad guy who was hiding nearby showed up and had to be restrained as well.

By then we were all scrambling on the ground in the dark with guns, gravel, blood, and bodies everywhere. We got things sorted out without anyone being shot or killed. No shots were ever fired. The point here is that even with highly trained and experienced police detectives, guns can get grabbed. If either had pulled out a knife, it is likely that the outcome would have been fatal for one or both. You will never see anything like this in a movie, but you might in real life.

CHAPTER TWELVE

KILLING PEOPLE

A s an experienced lawman, Wyatt Earp seldom carried a fire-arm at all when on duty. That was not uncommon in the old west. Old-timers out west did not carry handguns that often; they were cowboys, ranchers, and farmers with gardens and cattle to tend to if they wanted to eat. If cowboys had carried handguns constantly, you would find them on the ground all over the western plains and grasslands together with rusted-out tin cans, wheel rims, and other waste from old time settlements. They used rifles, not pistols, to kill predators, hunt, and fight wars. But unlike depictions in the movies, most people weren't packing heat. Most early American towns out west prohibited firearms from being taken into their jurisdictional limits because people were drinking alcohol in bars and other recreational establishments. In the 1800s, major Western towns like Tombstone, Deadwood, and Dodge City had some of the most restrictive gun laws in America, far more restrictive than they are today. By most estimates, fewer than 10% of Americans in frontier areas ever carried handguns. The common misconception that "God, guns, and guts" in the Old West made America is Hollywood fiction. Hardworking and industrious Americas built this country, but they were seldom armed.

Many police officers around the world today do not carry guns. Their concept is that most people will not shoot an unarmed person, especially a police officer. Having or displaying a gun changes the dynamics in all conflicts, even for law enforcement officers. Don't get me wrong, police do carry weapons of different types and they do need to use them at times, especially in America, but not as often as you might think. Not all that many officers will kill a person in their careers with their service weapons. According to Pew Research Data reported in February of 2017, 83% of Americans think police fire their weapons while on duty and many believe that they fire them more than once annually. In fact, only about one-quarter of police ever fire their weapons at another person in their entire career. Male police officers fire their weapons at other people three times as often as female officers (30% to 11%). White officers fire their weapons a third more often (31% to 21%) as non-white officers, and officers with military backgrounds discharge their weapons at others more often than those without military backgrounds (32% to 26%).

Some Americans have acquired guns in hopes that guns would make them seem, or even be more powerful or dangerous than they really are. This is part of American gun culture, but guns can't solve problems, especially for someone who is neither brave nor dangerous, and they can often make things worse.

If you had a firearm, could you pull the trigger? Some people could pull a trigger and kill you without batting an eye. Others could never do it. How can you tell?

As you would expect, the armed people I have faced in my career presented varying degrees of risk. Some of them were making a statement not associated with the gun at all. Many were just drunk and could not pose all that great of risk so long as I had some cover while implementing a better plan. Frankly, some police shootings have happened because the officers exposed themselves to risk unnecessarily and then had to shoot to protect themselves. This is not necessarily a "bad" shooting in the sense of being legally unjustified, but other options were available with proper cover. "Cover" just means hiding behind something, anything really, that a person cannot shoot through or can't see you through.

Part 1 of 5 - Dangerous People & Killing

In police work you meet people who are dangerous because they are drunk or on drugs, and sometimes ones who are cold-hearted killers. I have been faced with people pointing a gun at me many times. In one case, I was called to a domestic disturbance at a house in Barrow, Alaska. A drunk teenage girl had warrants for her arrest, and her family wanted her taken away. Her room was at the end of a hallway. She had pulled a short dresser to block the doorway and as I approached, she was closing the bolt of a hunting rifle. I drew my service revolver and was pulling up the slack in the trigger and taking aim when the family began screaming at me not to shoot her, "It's okay! She won't shoot you!" As I moved backward, I told them "Okay, then you be the ones to take the gun away from her." I was locked into the process of killing her and was only waiting for the barrel of her rifle to come up and level on me, then I would shoot. The family burst past me and they took the gun from her. She had delayed shooting me only because she could not get the breach closed because she was trying to load the rifle with the wrong size of ammunition.

That was a close call, and I think that if she could have, she would have shot me, but didn't, mostly because she was drunk. Few sober and rational people would try that unless they were trying to commit suicide by cop, which is a real thing. I am happy to this day that I did not have to kill her in front of her family. Things are often confusing and complex in situations like that.

Another time I was with an officer on duty, and I was in plain clothes setting up an electronic surveillance device that I had placed on a car. I was not armed at the time because I'd been crawling under cars getting the system set up and working and didn't want to lose or damage my handgun in the tight space under the car. To test the device, another officer and I hopped into an unmarked car and drove up and down the highway to calibrate the signal for use the next day. Suddenly, a truck passed us at high speed and skidded to a stop sideways in front of us, blocking the highway. A guy jumped out, aimed a handgun at us, and said, "Out of the car motherfuckers!" This came as a big surprise to us. I opened my door and dropped to the ground behind the door. My partner opened his door and with the door as cover, announced us as police officers and let the guy know he was the one who was about to die, not us. In just that fraction of a second, we could see that the driver was drunk and confused, and not confident in what he was doing. My partner did not shoot, and the bad guy slowly lowered his gun.

We handcuffed him and asked him what he was doing. He said he had been drinking at the bar and heard that someone was letting the air out of tires on cars parked at the bar, so he was out trying to find who was doing it. We booked him for second-degree assault.

Later, my partner almost quit police work because he felt he had failed a serious test that many officers will face in their careers: should he have shot a person? I can't tell you, even now, whether I would have shot the guy if I had been armed. It's hard to second guess these things. And yes, I know I should have been carrying a gun, but these things also happen sometimes. I urged my partner to consider he might have made a good decision;

that the risk was not as bad as it seemed, considering that he also had cover. (The bad guy ended up dying two years later when he drove that same truck, drunk on his ass, rolled it over, didn't have a seat belt on, and after falling halfway out the window, got crushed to death.) In my partner's case, I think that his decision at the time was the right answer. He stayed in police work and had an outstanding career as one of the best homicide detectives I ever met.

Judging risk is part of any armed encounter. A trained, experienced police officer has both a practical and legal advantage in a shooting situation that a private citizen does not.

Some people are dangerous, and you can feel it. On another occasion, I was part of an undercover bust of a cocaine dealer and the electronic bust signal went wrong. This can happen anytime radios are used. I got stuck, without cover, out in the open, only 20 feet from the bad guy who had his back to me. He was wearing a long black leather jacket. I was aiming my gun at him, near his heart-lung area, just below his shoulders, and identified myself as a police officer, but the rest of the bust team was slow in arriving. He looked over his shoulder and could see it was only me. He slowly looked over his shoulder with his right hand inside his left breast jacket pocket. He looked at me and then looked forward. He looked back again and right at my eyes. I could feel in an instant that he had a gun and was planning to kill me. I steadied my aim and began to tighten up on the trigger as I slowly exhaled to take the anticipated shot if I saw him turn with a gun to fire. He saw this and finally said, "Okay. Okay." He slowly took his hand off the gun that I had not yet seen and raised his hands. He announced that he had a gun, just to keep everything safe. My partners showed up and we took him into custody.

He was as cool as a cucumber. I asked him what he was thinking, and he told me he was planning to kill me, and in most cases, he would have, but when he looked back the second time, he could sense that I was in the process of shooting him and decided by the look in my eye that I would do it. He was right. I could also see this in him. He said that he could probably turn and shoot a cop before he or she ever fired a weapon. This is a pretty good assessment most of the time.

This guy was a cold calculating killer, and he didn't seem like his pulse rate even went up. This is what dangerous people are like. They will not threaten you. They will not display a gun in advance. They will not tell you that they have a gun. They will not act like a tough guy or say anything at all. They don't have to. A truly dangerous person does not need to try to convince you of it. It is part of the talkers-seldom-do and doers-seldom-talk thing. People who open-carry or wear guns out in public, screamers, protesters with military-style firearms and flags running around the streets are not the people you need to worry about. They are the talkers. They are generally just fools. Actual dangerous people never do silly things like that.

Part 2 of 5 - Courage (or Nerve) Under Fire

I have a few stories that illuminate some mental aspects of how you will feel the first time a person points a gun at you and some common psychological responses. Everyone will be different, but you should give all these some thought if you plan to arm yourself with a gun. Remember that if someone does point a gun at you, or you point one at someone else, either of you is possibly very close to the last few moments of your life. Everything will change in those moments. You will need to be prepared.

Some years ago, I attended a training class in California on what in police work we call a "Red Flag" event. These are deadly encounters that happened because the officers or detectives ignored or did not see warnings along the way that led up to bad events. Working undercover for many years, I saw many bad, complicated, unpleasant, and unplanned things happen. Often there were signs or indicators that we missed along the way that made things worse. Sometimes technological problems came from our carelessness. Inattention made these situations worse. Not properly checking a battery in a transmitter before an under-cover operation is a great example.

The instructor told a story of an undercover bust that he was involved in that went bad. He used the code word for the arrest team to come to his aid. Unfortunately, the arrest team did not hear the signal and the bad guy pushed the detective to the floor, pulled out his gun, and pulled the trigger. The automatic handgun misfired. He racked another round into the chamber. He pulled the trigger and it misfired again. After the third misfire, all of which happened in a few seconds, the detective was able to grab the bad guy, and as they struggled on the floor, the arrest team in the next room heard the noise, came in, and saved the day.

As this detective told the story about the moments in which he was sure that he was going to die, I could sense something in his voice and demeanor. He was struggling to express something difficult to say or convey. I felt a chill come over me. He was speaking in a language that I understood. During the break, I walked up to him to talk about a movie I once saw. Before I even was able to say the name of the movie, he said, "I know, I watch it over and over." The movie was "Fearless" starring Jeff Bridges, a movie that expresses this experience of being so near death and then surviving. A 1993 newspaper reviewer in the *Seattle Times* called the movie "Emotionally devastating." The movie captures this type of moment in a way I have seldom seen expressed in any medium. Watching it seems to help some people relive a traumatic moment and heal over time.

Three times in my life I was in situations where, like that instructor, I was completely sure that my life was over. Although I have had a number of people point guns at me in my police career, none of my three events involved firearms. I always felt that I was in control of the firearm encounters, but once I was lost in a storm on the ice in the Arctic Ocean; on another occasion, the engine of my airplane quit in the dark at a low altitude; and I once had a work-related medical emergency in which my heart stopped beating for a couple of minutes, but I stayed awake. In these three events, there seemed to be no way out. I entered a mental state where everything went into slow motion and milliseconds seem to last hours. I was not overly frightened at the time, and my actions remained deliberate and controlled. I felt my life had come to an end, and like I was merely an observer. I feel like I can resurrect that state of mind in a stressful situation. I would stay calm during the event, but the fear would come later, usually in a couple of days. If you have not had such an experience, this will be difficult to understand. If you survive one, and your fear comes later, that is what can be difficult to deal with. That is one effect of post-traumatic stress disorder that can be caused by a shooting or other near-death situation.

Some people find themselves in such a state of mental clarity when they enter a deadly shooting situation. Others do not respond this way at all and completely fall apart. Once I was working with a new police officer and we were waiting outside a house to arrest the suspect in a planned mass shooting at a school. After the arrest, we were going to do a search warrant on his residence. The officer leaned over to me in the bushes outside of the house in the dark and said, "I think I am going to piss my pants." Although I appreciated his candor, this is not what I wanted to hear from a fellow police officer in such a situation. Our team debriefed the event later, as we usually do, and after a long discussion, we all concluded that this was not the right line of work for him. He resigned from his commission and moved on to another life outside of police work.

These are just some examples of how you might act or respond when faced with a deadly encounter. This is just a warning for you to think about how you might experience a tactical situation. This could influence your decision about buying and displaying a weapon against another person.

Courage (nerve) never comes from the type of firearm you are using in a firefight. It does not come from the number of bullets you have in your gun or how cool your gun looks in person, online, or in a YouTube video. Although it is fine for a person to be afraid, it will be discipline, intelligence, and planning that creates the poise that protects someone in a gunfight. This cannot be replaced by firepower, flags, slogans, or gaudy displays of military-style weapons in public demonstrations.

Part 3 of 5 - Killing in Combat - More Difficult Than You Think

A fascinating statistic arose during WWI among fighter pilots. Only 15% of the pilots were accounting for a vast majority of all aerial kills (enemy airplanes being shot down). Initially, it was surmised that some of the pilots were just better pilots and better shots, but many pilots were engaging in significant "dog fights" or aerial combat with enemy fighters but did not fire their guns, or only fired them when no one was anywhere near where the bullets might hit.

Infantry soldiers had even worse results. Most would return from combat without having fired any bullets from their weapons. Soldiers were observed shooting above or away from the enemy.

Some political and military leaders without combat experience themselves were confounded. They failed to understand basic human nature, which they, as non-combatants, usually knew nothing about. By WWII, still only 15% to 20% of soldiers were willing to fire their weapons in combat. Even fewer were willing to intentionally kill another person. Tactical encounters and war, up close and personal, are very different from what John Wayne made it look like in the movies.

In truth, most people will not, or cannot, shoot or kill another person. Although people do indeed get shot and killed every day in America, it is usually drunk, mentally ill, deranged, or psychotic people who do the shooting and killing. Criminally psychotic people (only roughly 1% of the general population has this designation, and not even many of them kill others) tend to be attracted to crime, killing, and gangs. These people are not common in society, even though media stories sometimes make us think they are everywhere.

Battle-hardened gang members conduct a significant number of the shootings that occur in larger American cities. You are not likely to encounter or be assaulted by them in your home unless you live right in their neighborhoods. Even then, most of their shootings and killings occur within their organizations or between their members and rival gangs.

The problem for governments during wartime was getting soldiers to shoot their opponents. Leaders began to realize that the best way to do this was to objectify a person's opponent. If a soldier could not kill another person, then maybe it would be easier if he did not think of the other soldier as a person at all. Japanese became "nips" and Germans became "krauts." Opponents were portrayed as baby killers who raped women when they conquered territories. All sides of conflicts did this to motivate their soldiers. Not only were soldiers more willing to kill their opponents, but it also made war crimes and other abuses more likely and common. Unfortunately, the two went hand in hand.

I met a man once whose life exemplifies the effectiveness of objectifying an enemy. My friend Bernie Wemmer and I were part-time flight instructors in our spare time. Bernie's older brother, Reinhard Wemmer was also a pilot, and one day he went flying with us. Reinhard was much older than we were and had been a pilot in WWII in Germany. He showed us his logbook filled with German writing and swastika stamps. He was trained to fly fighter airplanes, but at the end of his training, Germany ran out of aviation fuel for its fighter aircraft, and he was put into the infantry. His first battle was the Battle of the Bulge, very near the end of WWII. He was severely wounded and was left on the battlefield to die. He had been told that if he were captured by Americans, they would torture and eat him. He was completely convinced by nationalist Nazi propaganda that Americans were cannibals. He told me that he believed this to be true because indoctrination and brainwashing were so strong in Germany. A dictatorial leadership culture based on a personality cult like Hitler's made this easy to do.

Reinhard Wemmer was captured by the American soldiers and given medical help and a chocolate bar. He told me that he never forgot that moment on the battlefield. He resolved that if he lived, he wanted to move to America. He felt that any country that treated its prisoners of war in such a way was a place he wanted to live and move his family to. He survived and did as he promised on the battlefield that day.

The point here is to show the lengths that governments must go to just to get soldiers to kill others. With new training and objectification of the enemy, shooting and killing rates rose to about 50% by the end of WWII. By the Korean War, that went up even higher. Not surprisingly, modern soldiers are de-sensitized to killing and their weapons can kill at further distances, even by remote control. However, society does not want to create just killers either. That is also a problem, in part because many soldiers transition into civilian police work. Soldiers are not trained to be problem solvers, and conversely, civilian police departments are concerned with the militarization of their forces. At the end of the Desert Storm War, the federal government gave surplus personnel carriers and armaments to local police departments. Some civilian police activity became too militaristic, leading to unintended deaths, and at least one municipal police department in Kern County, CA, was said to have sent its military equipment back. It is a delicate balance.

Part 4 of 5 – Automatic Overload – Fast Firing Weapons

Firing a military-style automatic or semiautomatic firearm, spewing out multiple shots per second, does not solve the problem of a shooter's needing mental discipline and physical precision to kill in a home defense situation. Military assault-style firearms are not magic. They do not think or fire on their own. No one will know exactly what they will do in an armed encounter until they face one in person. A military assault-style rifle cannot lessen this reality. A person could go to gun ranges with an AR-15-style gun for a thousand years and shoot a thousand rounds a day, but the mental aspect of the first time facing a gun aimed at him will be as complicated if he had not trained for it.

The other problem with fast-firing weapons, like an AR-15 or other military assault-style automatic firearm, is that the faster you fire, the more inaccurate you become. The noise and recoil will cause your heart and mind to race even more, and as you try to steady the impacts from the bullets, you fire more quickly to get your aim back, which does not work.

On March 19, 2022, a fight broke out between two persons at a car show and picnic in Dumas, Arkansas. As often happens with Americans, they pulled out their guns and began wildly firing at each other. When they were done, 28 people were hit by gunfire, including five children. One person died, but he was a bystander, not one of the armed persons in the gunfight. Although the exact types of weapons used have not yet been disclosed as of this writing, witnesses reported fast-firing weapons.

I have seen many people shooting military-style assault weapons in the forests over the last few years. Most were firing from the hip with the firearm held low and generally pointed at a target, using a stance like you'd see in a Rambo poster, not aiming carefully at all. They were not holding the gun to the shoulder like most people would a hunting rifle and were not looking down the barrel through the sights or a scope. They assume that the extra fast-firing bullets will make up for any inaccuracy on their part. This is almost always true when they fire these weapons in fully automatic mode. Americans do this because it is how they see them used in movies or on TV. But no rifle is even remotely accurate when fired in this way.

The military and police very seldom fire their weapons in fully automatic mode, but untrained people do it all the time. This is called, "spray and pray" and it never accomplishes what they want. Even firing a single round at a time can over-excite a shooter and throw his aim off. As a practical example, it is common for hunters with their first deer in their sights to freeze up and do nothing or fire wildly off-target; it's something called "Buck Fever." Their hearts are pounding and feel like they're going to jump out of their chests. They begin to sweat and shake to the point where they can hardly see straight. And this is just to shoot their first deer. More importantly, deer do not have guns that they are pointing and shooting back! If they did, few people would ever go hunting. An automatic weapon makes this much worse.

Part 5 of 5 - The Myths of Threats, Warning Shots and Wounding Shots

It is important to understand that if you are getting a gun for protection, you do not want to find out that you are incapable of firing it in self-defense until after you have pulled it out and are pointing it at someone. I will offer solutions for additional training later in Chapter Eighteen, "Advanced Training," but for now, here are some myths that you must avoid.

First, do not plan on having a stand-off with a gun like you may have seen in movies. If I am in a situation as a *private citizen* where it becomes completely necessary to kill an armed person with a gun, the last thing I want them to know is that I even have a firearm at all. Their first indication that I am armed with a firearm should come once they are already fatally wounded and are lying flat on the ground dying because I have already shot them in the heart or lungs.

You must never display your firearm to threaten someone with it. Do not display a gun until it is completely necessary, and all other options are exhausted. If it is truly time to shoot someone, then a fatal decision should have already been made, and you do not want your opponent to know that it is coming. Successful gunfights are not fair. There is no chivalry in them. Shooting and killing a person is not a sporting contest. After all other possible options are completely exhausted and there is nothing else left, it should be quick and lethal. But let me make one additional point completely clear:

Pointing a gun at someone is always the use of deadly force

That is why it is a felony to do so without proper cause. A civilian's unjustifiably pointing a gun at someone is, in and of itself, the crime of assault. It is entirely different with police and military because official forces are already assumed to be armed and authorized to use force.

Second, you must never fire a warning shot. No police officer is either trained or allowed to do this. It is fiction reserved entirely for the movies.

Third, you should never shoot someone to try to wound them without killing them. No police officer is trained or allowed to do this, either. Trying either of these will only get you or some innocent person killed. They also allow your opponent to shoot and kill you while they are only disabled. The Lone Ranger always shot his foe in the shoulder to disarm him, shooting with a pistol from a great distance, no less. That is a near impossibility, so please do not try to copy the Lone Ranger.

If you think otherwise, then you should never own a firearm for self-defense. Doing so will only get you or some innocent person killed. Bluffing or playing around when you are not ready or able to commit to using a firearm to kill someone will seldom work.

These statements will be highly controversial with some folks. Some conventional thinking is that you should pull out your gun whenever faced with intruders or potential threats to scare them away. Some will argue that guns can be used to bluff others into leaving or submitting. Gun sellers and right-wing media outlets love to propagate this foolish myth, but if you are not committed to killing that person at the very moment that you draw and point your weapon, it is a huge mistake. For every unprepared person who survives such an encounter, there will be far more who end up dead.

Arguments for using firearms to warn or wound often come from highly publicized stories about an individual encounter where someone pulls out a gun and the bad guy runs away. Usually, it is a woman in the story, just to make it even more dramatic. This plays on your mind to think of what may have happened to her without pulling out the gun. Some even cite statistics about interviews with bad guys who say they do not want to attempt a crime against an armed home or person, but this makes no sense. A bad guy wouldn't know you had a gun unless you had a sign on your home that said, "This home protected by Smith and Wesson." (I've seen such foolish welcome signs for burglars.) That creates more crime, not less. From my police experience, I know that guns are the third main item criminals want to steal from homes, only after large amounts of cash and illegal drugs like cocaine, heroin, and methamphetamine. Stealing other types of personal property falls far down the list. Handguns and military assault-style weapons stolen from burglaries have a high street value and are easy to sell.

Some people believe that the first person to bring out a gun and fire will win a gunfight. But it isn't necessarily the first bullet fired that wins a gunfight. The first fatal shot does. If you are faced with a person armed with a gun and they fire at you, they will often miss with the first or first few shots. You will always want to use any available cover to protect yourself whenever possible. Some cover also gives you the opportunity to take your time and fire a fatal shot the first time you shoot a bullet.

Yes, a gun can stop a crime, but only if the shooter is trained and capable of killing the offender. Casual and improper training will not work. Does this seem harsh, or is it something you are not comfortable with? Good. These are things you need to understand in advance of getting a gun for protection. This is what using a gun to defend yourself will be like.

CHAPTER THIRTEEN

CHOOSING YOUR FIREARM

There are thousands of different firearms available in America today, so let's look at some you might want to think about to either purchase and use, or just to understand better.

To begin with, if you are buying a gun to store in case our country is someday overthrown by a dictatorship, then your selection might be different from a firearm purchased today for home defense. I address that in Chapter 21, "What to Hide and Where to Hide It." In this chapter, I will discuss firearms selected for home defense.

Part 1 of 4 - All Quiet on the Western Front—The Rifle

On the night of June 24, 1982, I was sitting in the closet of a bedroom in a house in a rural area southeast of Seattle. I was with a police sergeant from another agency, and we were waiting for a man named Robert Hughes to return to his home in the dark.

Earlier that day Hughes had shot King County Sherriff's Deputy Samuel Hicks as he and another deputy drove up to the Hughes home to talk to him about a murder investigation. Detective Hicks was hit in the abdomen with a .308 hunting rifle from a long distance away. The deputies turned their vehicle around and left the scene, but the wound was mortal, and Hicks died on the way to the hospital.

Local law enforcement officers went on stake-out to catch Hughes. He had fled on foot. My partner and I were dropped off so there would be no vehicles near the house to give away our presence. That was a long night for me, hiding in a closet with my shotgun (you will notice, not a rifle). Hughes did not return to the house that night. He had buried himself close by in some woods where he had pulled leaves over himself to conceal his location. A police K-9 dog smelled him and alerted the handlers the next day. That's where he was arrested without any shots being fired or anyone else being hurt.

The point here is to illuminate both the danger and the utility of what police officers call a long-gun, or what most people think of as a hunting rifle. At any distance over 50 yards, nothing is a match to a rifle with a scope, a good rest to prop it on, and some cover or concealment. One person with a hunting rifle and a scope could hold off a small army. A single shot bolt action rifle with a scope is by far the most devastatingly accurate firearm at more than 100 yards, especially if it is shooting high-velocity medium-caliber bullets. All the handguns, un-scoped AR-15s, and shotguns in the world are no match at longer distances.

People who are thinking of buying a firearm for self-defense in their homes seldom think of a hunting rifle. This is partly because of the popular concept that military-style assault weapons are what everyone else has and that you need all those bullets for self-defense, but this is an error.

Rather than using an automatic weapon in a hostage or barricaded suspect situation, law enforcement generally will try to deploy a sniper with a long rifle and a scope. This is the only way of assuring accuracy, and the sniper will seldom fire more than one single shot to end the encounter.

The history of what you might think of as a "sniper" goes back at least 150 years in the U.S. During the Civil War, snipers got good at killing soldiers at long distances. One such documented kill happened at over 4,000 feet, just under a mile, during the battle at Fort Sumpter in April of 1861. Modern military snipers have documented kills at 10,000 feet, or nearly two miles. Long single-shot firearms are dangerous and accurate weapons.

Military snipers have become adept at using rifles as powerful as .50 caliber weapons with a high degree of accuracy. Civilians now buy these weapons if they want to. I see them from time to time in the woods, but they are extremely expensive to shoot, and untrained private citizens can injure themselves with serious head wounds due to their recoil. I saw one unprepared shooter out in the woods two years ago fire a .50 caliber scoped rifle. The recoil drove the scope into his head, splitting his scalp and underlying tissue and causing profuse bleeding. He was unconscious for several minutes, then obviously affected by concussive brain trauma. You would never need a rifle this powerful for any reason.

Although I have pointed out that movies and the internet are the worst possible places to get accurate information about firearms, there is a scene in the popular 1930 WWI book and film, "All Quiet on the Western Front" that is accurate. It is the final scene of probably one of the best anti-war movies ever made. At the beginning of the movie, a group of young German students is fooled into leaving school and signing up to fight in the German army. Initially, they are excited to go to war, but they eventually learn the realities of what war really means, and by the end of the movie, they are all dead. The final soldier in this original group is killed by a sniper with a long rifle as he is reaching out just beyond the berm of his trench.

A close friend recently told me, "My dad's childhood buddy was killed by a sniper in Germany, just after peace had been declared, at the end of WWII." The sniper saw this exposed soldier and had not received the notice of hostilities ending. Exposure, when a sniper was in the area, could mean almost instant death in combat, due to the accuracy of rifles.

An advantage to using a hunting rifle for home defense is that it is much less likely to be stolen from a home, as opposed to a handgun or military-style assault weapon. Young people, gangs, and burglars seldom want them. They are too unwieldy to transport in secret and are not easy to sell for much. This alone makes them safer to have in a home. A bolt action hunting rifle is far more accurate at 100 to 300 yards compared to a handgun, and even much more accurate than an AR-15 automatic assault-style rifle that does not have a scope. Hunting rifles also shoot bullets that expand when hitting a person and do extensive damage with a single shot.

What type of hunting rifle might be good for protection in your home? Pretty much anything that can accurately kill a deer, moose, or elk would work well in killing a person. There are lots of older WWI and WWII surplus weapons on the market and people have hunted with them for decades. They tend to be larger caliber, like a .308 or 30-06. You can tell they are old because they have wooden rather than plastic stocks. I would avoid older worn-out weapons from this era because many overused ones have worn-out rifling so are no longer accurate. A good gunsmith can tell you if they are still operable and safe.

Modern hunting rifles are often of smaller caliber but use a higher velocity bullet, or "round." Most are single-shot bolt-action rifles that are reliable and seldom misfire, but some come in semi-automatic versions. One such firearm is called a .270 Winchester round. Another is a .243. The .270 and .243 are not specific rifles, but rather, they are named for the bullets they fire. Different companies make rifle models that fire this .270 round and they cost from about $350 to over $1,000. Some are made with synthetic stocks which are simple and virtually indestructible.

A hunting rifle is also effective because of how the bullet performs after it leaves the muzzle of the firearm. Hunting rifle bullets come in different weights, but one of the most popular is the 130-grain round which travels at around 3,000 feet per second when measured at the muzzle. Their velocity makes them excellent for shooting long distances—they reach their targets before gravity has time to bring them down--but are also very powerful at close range. Standard hunting rounds of ammunition have soft points and a single one will cause significant damage if used in self-defense at close range.

Part 2 of 4 – A Shotgun Approach

The most terrifying sight that an intruder in your home will ever see is the muzzle of a shotgun aimed at the center of his chest. A single shot will be unsurvivable. If he has come to kill you, it is the last thing he will ever see. It makes no difference what he is armed with. There will be no shootout, just a killing.

The relatively short range and width of the blast from a shotgun will obviate the inaccuracy of your trying to aim a rifle or handgun when you are scared. Just point a shotgun in the right direction, and if you can just pull the trigger, you will kill everybody in its deadly path.

A huge setback to using a shotgun is collateral damage from its blast. That is why police do not use shotguns in shopping malls, schools, or other crowded situations. In your home or a confined situation, this is less an issue.

I often carried a 12-guage Mossberg stainless steel Marine Corps shotgun while I carried out dangerous search warrants. Today, Mossberg sells a Tactical 590A1 model that the police and military often use. They are the ultimate tactical weapon, and even its presence convinces people that resistance or shooting back is pointless.

Another benefit of using a shotgun for home safety is that it is easier than other firearms to learn how to use. After some basic training, you just point and shoot. There is no scope to keep sighted in or to knock out of alignment. Well-made shotguns are resilient and resistant to climate and corrosion.

Firing 00 Buckshot, a 12-gauge shotgun is a weapon that can stop anything or anyone in its path within 50 yards. In the 20' hallway of your home, nothing will survive it. This weapon has "knockdown" power. It can pick up the bad guy, throw him back a distance, and flatten him on his back. No one shot this way will be firing back at you.

Shotguns are not a weapon of choice for self-defense for most people, but I think they are the ultimate home defense weapon. They are not considered cool, and street gangsters don't want to be seen with them. They are seen as stodgy, akin to your grandfather's old duck-hunting gear.

The first person I ever saw shot with a 12-gauge shotgun was in 1983 when I was a police officer for the North Slope Borough Department of Public Safety in Alaska. I had only been there for a week and got a call about a shooting in an apartment. At that time, we had shootings and gun calls frequently. Barrow was likely the homicide capital of the known world at that time. As we arrived, we had to sneak down a long hallway. This was scary on a gun call, but each doorway was indented a little, so we did have some cover along the way. We were looking for a room halfway down the hall, so not an easy approach.

Coming to the door, I used a small round rear-view mirror like the one from a car to look inside. I didn't want to get shot through a doorway sticking my head around a corner to look. My two partners and I probably took 10 minutes to approach the door and found that it was unlocked. I lay as flat on the floor as I possibly could while my partners covered me. I reached the mirror around and inside the door. I could see a person lying on the floor and no one else inside. Then the other two officers entered the room while I watched from my low point and covered them with my handgun. Once we determined that the shooter was not inside, we found that the guy on the floor was dead from a shotgun wound to the center of his chest.

Interestingly, the killer had tried to kill two of us about an hour earlier. Barrow had a serious alcohol problem back then and drunks would try to ambush the police. It was almost like a local sport. All our Chevy Suburban patrol vehicles had bullet holes in them except one, too new to be shot up yet. People shot the police vehicles so often that we just put square pieces of blue tape over the bullet hole instead of repairing them. When I was in orientation a week earlier and was told about all the square blue tape pieces on the vehicles, I thought my trainers were kidding me until I looked under the hood. Seeing the bullet holes from the inside, I found that it was true. I also found big cardboard boxes with black rubber things in them in the back of the patrol vehicles. When I asked what they were, I was told they were body bags. Again, I thought they were just kidding. I'd never seen a body bag up to that point in my career.

Earlier we had gotten a call that was like so many others. They went like this: The police dispatcher would answer a call and the caller would just say, "Send one quick!" The dispatcher would ask who was calling and the caller would say, "You know who this is!" The dispatcher would say that she did not know (this was long before caller ID) and ask again for the caller's name. The caller would say a name and the dispatcher would ask the caller's location. The caller would answer, "You know where I live!" as if shocked that the dispatcher did not already know. The dispatcher would ask again, "Where are you calling from?" and because there were no street or house signs, the answer could be somewhat convoluted. Once the dispatcher established a location, she'd ask what the problem was, and the caller would hang up.

This was usually an ambush. Typically, an officer approaching the door would be faced with several drunk people with hunting rifles who would then shoot. Even driving up to the house would get us shot, or at least we would need more pieces of blue tape for the bullet holes in the vehicle. We would sneak up on foot to the house and watch until someone walked away, and once he or she was safely away from the door or windows, we'd ask if everything inside was okay. If the answer was yes, then we would cancel the call and go on to something else.

In this case, the bad guy got tired of waiting to shoot me and my partner and went to the house of the superior court judge to kill him instead, but the judge was on vacation in Hawaii. Now even more frustrated, the shooter went to the apartment of his ex-brother-in-law, whom he also disliked, and found the brother-in-law drunk on the floor, so shot him in the chest with a 12-gauge shotgun. He shot at close range with birdshot, a popular goose and duck hunting round. The victim probably never even knew he was shot. The birdshot cartridge opened upon entering his chest and the shot spread throughout his body cavity and went all the way to his back. But since it was only birdshot, it did not pierce his skin and exit out his back. When we rolled him over, we saw a one-foot circle of small bumps of birdshot just on the inside of his skin. Everything else inside his chest was liquid mush that poured out the hole in the front of his chest when we rolled him over.

Once we completed our investigation, the Sergeant told me to go get a body bag out of the back of the Suburban. They were not kidding about that. I soon found that we used them all the time. I inquired if a doctor or medical examiner should come and pronounce the person dead. The Sergeant said, "Are you stupid? You can't see that this guy is dead?" This seemed logical enough, albeit different from my earlier law enforcement experience in Washington State, where a medical examiner had to pronounce a person dead. I got a body bag out of the vehicle, and we zipped the guy up inside. We dragged him down the stairs, stuffed him into the back seat of the patrol vehicle, and took him to the hospital in Barrow. We put him into their freezer so he could be sent to Fairbanks the next morning for an autopsy.

In my year on the North Slope of Alaska during 1983 and 1984, I had more tactical shooting and dead body calls of one sort of another than most cops would ever get in an entire career in the lower 48. Many officers attracted by the remarkable salary lasted less than a day or two when they found out what our work was like. Some toughed it out and did their year, which is what the North Slope Borough Department of Public safety asked of officers they hired. A small number stayed and never left. It was a great place to observe the natural world, but also a sadly brutal world of drugs and alcohol that was devastating an ancient culture of people who were being confronted with all aspects of middle-class American civilization at once. Over time, locals made possession and sales of alcohol a crime, and that helped.

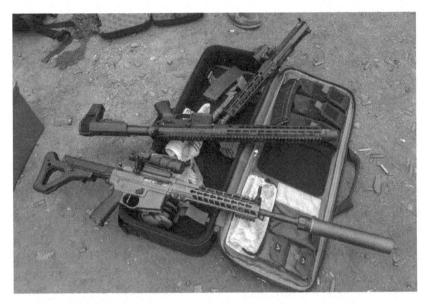

Military Assault-style firearms, one with a silencer.

Part 3 of 4 —What's an AR-15 and Why Not to Buy One for Home Defense

Precisely, an AR-15 is a rifle originally designed and manufactured by the Armalite Rifle company. Colt now owns the trademarked name, "AR-15." Its patents that form its design have expired, so other manufacturers may copy its design, but they can't use that exact name. They have to say "AR-15 style" firearm, or words to that effect, in their advertising. The name is reserved for the trademark owner, like "Scotch Tape" for the 3-M company, but "mending tape" for other makers, or "Daisy BB Gun" for Daisy Outdoor Products, but "Daisy-like BB gun" for others.

The AR-15-style gun isn't just a single rifle. The name refers to a large group of weapons that most commonly fire the 5.56x45mm round or the .223 Remington cartridge. It can be chambered for many other rounds as well. There are also 25 different models of

this weapon made by at least 15 different companies. Many owners buy a long list of modifications from online retailers that allow
them to turn these weapons into virtually thousands of different
individual styles. Building a new one with parts from a variety of
different sources from online sites is a common way of making the
firearm without any background checks being done. Today there
are hundreds of websites encouraging and explaining how to do
this.

Between 1994 and 2004, sales and possession of military
assault-style firearms were illegal. Then the law expired, and these
weapons became available to anyone who could legally purchase
a firearm. One of the most popular guns in America today is the
formerly banned AR-15-style military assault-style weapon. The
Russians and Chinese have their own versions, like the AK-47 and
the SKS.

Some years ago, the Israeli Uzi was all the rage, and everyone
wanted one. The Uzi is a short, compact submachine gun. Many
people thought that it was the standard issue weapon for the Israeli
army, but it was not. I have shot these at a firing range. I tried ones
that we took from bad guys, and I found them to be remarkably
inaccurate at distances beyond a few feet. They became popular
because you could spray 1,500 rounds a minute with them. And
of course, they looked cool. Make no mistake about it, they can be
dangerous, but you will generally hit more non-target things and
people with one than what you intended to hit.

The AK-47 became the standard of the automatic weapon
industry around the world. In 1947, the inventor, Mikhail Kalash-
nikov, managed to create a weapon that could be dropped on the
side of the road, be buried in the mud for several weeks, get run
over by a Jeep, and somehow still come out firing most of the time.
It didn't seem to matter what happened to them; they kept working. Around the same time, in the early 1950s, American military

assault weapons were prone to breakdowns and were performing poorly in bad weather or muddy conditions. They needed constant attention just to keep them firing. Armies around the world preferred the AK-47 to American models. They still do today, and so do criminal street gangs in America. They loved the perceived simplicity and reliability over American-made weapons, although current American models are more reliable than the older ones were.

AK-47s are also much cheaper than American-made fully automatic weapons. The Russians made a gazillion of them in the early days, then chambered them to accept NATO ammunition, reportedly so that they could fire any cache of ammunition captured from NATO members. This makes a lot of sense in war. Ak-47s are easy to find and buy. There are estimated to be over 100 million of them in the world today, and in 2012, Americans were buying far more of them than AR-15s. For a while, it was all the rage to own one.

The SKS was designed as a semi-automatic weapon only and was made by the Russians as well. It is generally seen as an inferior weapon to the AK-47. The Chinese made and shipped over 15 million of them. They are inexpensive and easy to find.

"Military-style assault-type" weapons are deeply polarizing to Americans. Some people love them, and others see them as the poster child of what is wrong with American gun culture and crime. Emotion tends to replace facts in this debate.

"Military assault-style weapons" are primarily offensive weapons, designed to kill or injure groups of people quickly, especially in some of the ways that Americans modify them after they leave the factory. However, it is not assault-style weapons, but rather handguns that are used in most shootings in America today. Although not all that common, the most notable use of military assault-style weapons in a mass shooting was in Las Vegas in 2017.

The accuracy of these weapons, especially when fired in full auto mode, is not high. Even at seven or eight rounds being fired each second, they will be amazingly inaccurate, except when firing into a crowd of people. Hitting a lot of people crammed into a dense crowd does not mean that this was an accurate weapon.

People think that the more bullets a weapon has, the better it will be, but if you need more than the first two bullets, you are at a significant disadvantage and are now very likely to lose the encounter. That is how police are trained. At close range, they fire two shots at center mass (the middle of a person's upper torso) and then assess whether the threat is neutralized.

At longer ranges, law enforcement officers do not empty a 30 or 40 round clip with a fully automatic firearm like in the movies. Neither do the military. If they did, they would rarely hit anything, no matter how many rounds they fired.

Automatic weapons are devastatingly dangerous in the hands of police officers or members of the military who train with them often. You would not want to oppose a Navy Seal Team member or Army Ranger with one in a dark building. Your chances of surviving or winning that encounter would be slim to none. However, your peril is not due to the weapon, but rather to the sophisticated training and discipline of the shooter.

An AR-15 is designed to be an offensive weapon, not a defensive one for home protection. Police don't use them to defend their police stations from the inside like a home. They would use a shotgun for that.

AR-15 style weapons are expensive to shoot because they can fire so many rounds quickly, especially if they are fully automatic. Most of these weapons on fully auto cost at least $3.50 per second (That's $210.00 per minute) to shoot cheap ammunition. Using much of this cheaper ammo will destroy the weapon in a short amount of time. Better ammo is twice that price.

Further, the skills necessary to be proficient with one of these will take more time and work than most Americans are willing to invest. I define "proficiency" as a level of knowledge and comfort that allows for no mistakes in handling a tactical encounter against an armed person. There are far simpler firearm options that require less training, attention, and money for home defense.

Once a bullet leaves the muzzle of a firearm, it does not care what it has been fired from. It's just a bullet traveling through the air. Its accuracy and deadliness do not depend on how many bullets are back in the gun behind it. Ultimately, all that matters is getting it into the air and determining where it will land. In the right hands, an AR-15 style assault weapon is a deadly offensive weapon, but good ones are expensive and more complicated to use and maintain.

If your goal is to buy and possess an offensive weapon to give to a militia or a resistance operation against a dictatorship in the future, then some of these might be very useful, and I will discuss how to acquire and store them in Chapter 21, "What to Hide and Where to Hide It."

Part 4 of 4 - Handguns

Handguns for home defense are popular because many are small and easy to conceal. Some criminal organizations like to use them as murder weapons because, at very close range, they can be quiet, and because they are small and concealable. But a .22, .32, .25, or other smaller caliber handgun, in my opinion, is worthless in self-defense situations at a range outside of a couple of feet. For the most part, a .22 handgun will wound, but not kill unless discharged directly into a person's skull at point-blank range. I have seen a .22 bullet shot into a person's head that passed through one side of the skull, and instead of going out the other side, just ran around the inside like a racetrack, doing damage on the way. Some automatic handguns are very small. These smaller ones also fire small rounds, and being almost hopelessly inaccurate beyond a few feet away, may not do all that much damage.

At a few feet away from an intruder, a 9mm, .38 Special or .357 magnum will be fatal with a single shot or two to the center body mass if the bullet hits the heart or lung area. They will also be very noisy. At further distances, the .38 Special rounds, and even some 9mm ammunition, are not as effective.

I am not including photos of any of this, because I don't think that forensic pictures are necessary for you to understand any of this. However, if you are interested, or just like to watch Crime Scene CSI or programs like that on TV, it is easy to look at the entrance, exit, head, heart, and lung wounds on TV programs or with a simple online search.

As a police detective I found crime scenes fascinating. Investigating them was always an interesting part of my job. I was not alone in this. Crime scene programs have become some of the most popular shows on TV. I don't watch many of them nowadays because I have seen most similar scenes in person over my years in police work. But from some that I have seen, I can tell you that many programs are pretty accurate; they must have tracked actual cases or had police and forensic scientific advisors. You are lucky that you can't smell crime scenes on TV or online.

As a practical matter, a revolver will virtually never misfire. If you pull the trigger of a double-action handgun, it will shoot a round of ammunition in the direction it is pointed every time. An automatic will usually work, but not unless it is maintained to a high standard.

Two of the best revolvers ever made are the Model 66 and Model 19 Smith & Wesson .38 Special or .357 handguns with 4-inch to 6-inch barrels. Police often use the shorter 2.5-inch

barrel models in undercover roles because they are easily concealable but are still very powerful. These were carried by the FBI
in years past. A .357 is chambered the same as a .38 Special so
you can shoot either bullet from the same gun. One bullet is just
shorter and less powerful than the other.

The Smith & Wesson Model 66 Combat Magnum with a
4.25-inch barrel is, in my opinion, the most accurate and reliable
handgun in the world. It is stainless steel and can come with a
synthetic, or tactical grip. This makes it is easy to hold onto in all
weather conditions. It is virtually indestructible and fires 100% of
the time. I carried one during much of my police career. I could
almost always shoot a perfect, or very close to a perfect score on
a police shooting range with one. Nothing else came as close. I
also often carried the 2.5-inch Model 19 Smith & Wesson revolver
when I wanted something more concealable, or when I was working undercover. I could wear it in an ankle holster. It could also
fire both the .38 Special and .357 magnum rounds. Although less
accurate than the Model 66, in some cases like in undercover
work, it was much easier to have on my person or close by when I
did not want it discovered or seen.

Advocates of automatic handguns will tell you that they
are superior weapons. This is not always the case. Don't get me
wrong, there are many fine semi-automatic handguns, and in full
disclosure, I also carried one: A German-made Heckler & Koch
.40 caliber S&W handgun. I carried it in the last few years that I
was a detective commander. I had several police-issued 12 round
clips that carried a particularly nasty hollow point round that was
only available to law enforcement at the time. This was the most
accurate and reliable semiautomatic handgun that I ever shot or
carried, but in the end, I could outshoot it every time with my
Model 66 Smith & Wesson revolver at a range. Both are excellent
offensive and defensive weapons.

In years past I had been issued 9mm semiautomatic police firearms, but personally deemed earlier versions inadequate for police work. Whenever I could get away with it, like many other knowledgeable police officers, I put it away and carried better weapons. Detectives could usually get away with this, but often patrol officers could not; most detectives had different rules and flexibility on what weapons they carried if they had properly qualified with them at the range and would maintain them.

I can't tell you how many times I saw or had 9mm police handguns jam or misfire. Newer ones are better than those early ones. The worst was the early 9mm Glock, a firearm I considered to be almost entirely worthless. A lot of guys loved them. I think mostly because they were deemed to be cool. Of all the hair-brained ideas, Glock put the safety in the trigger itself to make it easier to fire. Once the trigger was partly pulled, the safety, a small lever in the trigger, released as the trigger came back, allowing the gun to be fired. That was unlike conventional safeties that lock the internal parts of the firearm from a lever away from the trigger, on the outside of the action. Having the safety of a handgun in the trigger is a bad idea.

The older 9mm Glocks caused too many workplace injuries and death claims, and after several police officers were killed with their own service weapons in quick succession, many were removed from police work.

A proper handgun should have a safety that is difficult for a bad guy to figure out quickly (if it has one at all – many do not). If they got my H&K away from me, if the safety were on, it is highly unlikely that they could have gotten it to fire in less than a minute or two. On that gun, the user must look at and read and understand the message on the side of the gun to get it to work.

I once visited a good friend in police work at his office and noticed that he had a hand grenade on his desk. Looking closer,

I could see a big dent in the front that looked like the shape of a bullet. My friend was a commander, but also a SWAT team member. I asked him about the item. He told me that "Chuck," another member of his SWAT team, who was a good friend of each of us, had accidentally shot him with a live round during training at Fort Lewis, a local Army facility. The bullet hit the hand grenade that was hanging on his ballistic vest. Even though all guns had to be carefully "cleared" before the exercise, meaning they had to have no live rounds in them, Chuck left a bullet round in his semi-automatic handgun, and accidentally fired it. Chuck, who had been a military sniper, was famous for taking "headshots" at close range, something that was discouraged in police work, and not often done because a person's head is a much smaller target than the center body mass in the chest area. Fortunately, this was not a headshot. Instead, the bullet hit the hand grenade, smashing it without setting it off, and crushing it into the ballistic vest the Commander was wearing. No one was badly hurt, and there were indeed repercussions for the accident, as there always must be in police work, but no one got fired. Even highly trained officers on a SWAT team can make mistakes with semi-automatic weapons. This could not have happened with a revolver. It did, however, make a great desk ornament!

Simplicity, reliability, proper caliber, and power, far outweigh the need for more complex and higher capacity firearms. Further, properly trained persons with a revolver can re-load it almost as quickly as an automatic handgun with the use of a device called a "speed loader." If necessary, with speed loaders, I can re-load six bullets into a revolver in three seconds without looking, and in about two seconds with visual contact.

CHAPTER FOURTEEN

PERSONAL FIREARM SAFETY

It is very important to know some basic rules on firearm safety. Understand them before you buy one and bring it home. It is easy to get a copy of an owner's manual and to read it ahead of time. You can almost always get one online for your new gun purchase. Heed all warnings, of which there will be many. Gun manufacturers want you to have this information on the specific weapon you buy from them.

Here is a typical generic warning for a firearm that you can find online (this approximates the format of many warnings):

Read the instructions and warnings in this manual BEFORE any use of this firearm.

WARNING
READ THESE INSTRUCTIONS AND WARNINGS WITH SERIOUS CAUTION. BE SURE YOU UNDERSTAND THESE

INSTRUCTIONS AND WARNINGS BEFORE USING THIS FIREARM IN ANY WAY. FAILURE TO READ THESE INSTRUCTIONS AND TO FOLLOW THESE WARNINGS MAY RESULT IN SERIOUS INJURY OR DEATH TO YOU AND OTHERS OR DAMAGE TO PROPERTY.

This SAFETY & INSTRUCTION MANUAL should always accompany any firearm and be transferred with it upon change of ownership or when presented to another person for their use of the weapon. A copy of the SAFETY & INSTRUCTION MANUAL is available FREE via download at www.[manufacturers website].com or upon request from:

[gun manufacturers name]
CUSTOMER SUPPORT CENTER & Company address
TEL.: 1-800-555-5555, ext. 5555 E-mail: email address

YOUR SAFETY& RESPONSIBILITIES

SAFETY IS YOUR RESPONSIBILITY

At home, in the field, at the range, or anywhere, the first concern of every firearm owner should be safety. Apply the following safety rules in every situation, with any kind of firearm. If you feel uncertain about any operational aspects of your firearm, please contact [the gun manufacturer's name and phone number are usually here] before proceeding with its operation.

If you are unfamiliar with firearms, you should seek formal training before using your revolver.

WARNING: YOU MUST FOLLOW ALL OF THESE SAFETY RULES TO ENSURE THE SAFE USE OF THIS OR ANY FIREARM.

THE FAILURE TO FOLLOW THE INSTRUCTIONS AND WARNINGS IN THIS MANUAL COULD CAUSE SERIOUS PERSONAL INJURY OR DEATH TO YOU OR OTHERS AND DAMAGE TO PROPERTY.

As a firearm owner, you accept a serious responsibility. How seriously you take this responsibility can be the difference between life and death. There is no excuse for careless or abusive handling of your firearm. At all times handle your firearm with intense respect for its power and potential danger to you and others.

_ _

There are usually triangle warnings of all kinds to catch your attention. And exclamation points throughout!!! Some of this is in bright colors, just so you pay attention and take this all seriously. The manuals usually include the maker's phone number, mailing address, and email, just in case something is not clear. Here are the key basic rules that you need to know and obey:

1. ALWAYS KEEP YOUR FIREARM POINTED IN A SAFE DIRECTION. Don't point a firearm at anyone or anything you do not intend to shoot and kill, whether it is loaded or not. This is particularly important when loading, unloading or disassembling the gun. ALWAYS control the direction of the firearm in all conditions no matter where you are.

2. ALWAYS TREAT EVERY FIREARM AS IF IT IS LOADED AND WILL FIRE. Do not take anyone's word that the firearm is unloaded – always check for yourself. Never pass your firearm to another person until the cylinder or action is open and you visually check yourself that it is unloaded. Keep your firearm unloaded and safely stored when not in use. (There will be debate about quick access to a firearm for self-defense at home, but this is the general rule)

3. NEVER PLACE YOUR FINGER INSIDE THE TRIGGER GUARD OR ON THE TRIGGER UNLESS YOU INTEND TO FIRE. Ensure that no other objects can reach inside the trigger-guard or can touch the trigger because they could snag and pull the trigger.

4. ALWAYS BE SURE OF YOUR TARGET AND WHAT IS BEYOND IT. Always be sure of where any bullet can possibly strike and shoot only where there is a safe backstop free of obstructions, water, or other surfaces which can cause ricochets. Be sure your bullet will stop behind your target without going through. Bullets can glance off many hard surfaces like rocks. Be aware that bullets can ricochet off the surface of water and travel in unpredictable directions with considerable velocity. Never fire randomly into the sky.

5. NEVER CROSS OBSTACLES SUCH AS FENCES OR STREAMS WITH A LOADED FIREARM. Always make certain your firearm is unloaded before crossing a fence, climbing a tree, jumping a ditch, or negotiating any type of obstacle of any kind where you cannot fully and completely control your firearm. The trigger could get snagged and fire the weapon.

6. SAFE GUN HANDLING IS YOUR RESPONSIBILITY AT ALL TIMES. Firearms are dangerous and can cause serious injury or death if they are misused or used inappropriately. Safety must be the prime consideration of anyone who owns or handles firearms. Accidents are the result of violating the rules of safe gun handling and common sense. Firearm safety training is available and necessary. Contact your firearms dealer, law enforcement agency, local sportsman's club, etc. for availability.

7. YOU ARE RESPONSIBLE FOR THE FIREARM AT ALL TIMES. In owning a firearm, you must undertake full-time responsibility for your firearm's safety and security. You must protect yourself and all others against injury or death from misuse of the firearm 24 hours a day.

8. FIREARM SECURITY IS YOUR RESPONSIBILITY. You must secure firearms safely from children and unauthorized users. Your firearm should always be kept unloaded and locked when not in use. (Again, some argue for quicker access, but this is a basic rule) A lock is sometimes provided with your firearm for this purpose. Never assume that the use of this lock is sufficient to safely secure your firearm. Check the quality of the locking device yourself. You must always evaluate your situation and employ the security systems that meet your needs and prevents children and unauthorized users from gaining access to your firearm. Do not assume that the lock that comes with a gun is fully adequate and do your research. See Chapter 16, Firearm Safety in Your Home.

9. APPROPRIATE USE FOR YOUR FIREARM MEANS USING YOUR FIREARM FOR LEGAL PURPOSES. Use

your firearm for target shooting, hunting, and _lawful_ resistance of deadly crime in progress in your home. It is your responsibility to ensure that you are following all applicable laws and ordinances regarding the use of your firearm. To aim your firearm at another person without legal justification to do so is the crime of assault.

10. NEVER RELY ON MECHANICAL SAFETY FEATURES ALONE. Only your safe gun-handling habits will ensure the safe use of your firearm. This is your responsibility. Don't rely on the internal mechanical safety of the gun as your only security device.

11. ALWAYS SAFELY STORE AND SECURE YOUR FIREARM. Safe and secure storage of your firearm is one of your most important responsibilities. It is a full-time responsibility. See Chapter 16, "Firearm Safety in Your Home."

12. NEVER KEEP AMMUNITION IN THE SAME LOCATION AS THE FIREARM. Store each in a separate and secure place. (This is a basic rule, a good starting place.). See Chapter 16 on Firearms Safety at Home and Chapter 21, "What to Hide and Where to Hide It."

13. ALWAYS WEAR EYE PROTECTION THAT IS SPECIFIED FOR USE WITH FIREARMS. Wear eye protection every time you handle your firearm for target practice, cleaning, and maintenance. A billed baseball cap also can help protect you from being hit by hot brass being ejected from your firearm after you fire it.

14. ALWAYS WEAR EAR PROTECTORS THAT ARE SPECI-FIED FOR USE WITH FIREARMS. Use ear protection every time you discharge your firearm. Make sure that others in the vicinity of where you will be shooting do so as well. That includes other users at the range.

15. NEVER USE ALCOHOL OR DRUGS BEFORE OR WHILE SHOOTING. Do not use your firearm if you are on any pre-scription or over-the-counter medication that could impair your mental state or reflexes, or any alcohol of any kind, which impairs, even slightly, your mental or physical ability. Not even one sip of alcohol is okay. Don't have it close by when using firearms.

16. ALWAYS HAVE ADEQUATE VENTILATION. Discharging firearms in poorly ventilated areas, cleaning firearms, or han-dling ammunition may result in exposure to lead and other substances that are known to cause birth defects, repro-ductive harm, and other serious physical injuries. Review the warnings and labels for all ammunition and cleaning products carefully. Wash hands and clothes thoroughly after exposure.

17. BEFORE HANDLING ANY FIREARM, UNDERSTAND ITS OPERATION. Not all firearms operate the same. Famil-iarize yourself with the mechanical features of any firearm you intend to use. If you feel uncertain about any opera-tional aspects of your firearm, please contact the manufac-turer before its use or get professional training by a qualified trainer.

18. NEVER ALLOW A FIREARM TO BE USED BY INDIVID-
     UALS WHO DO NOT UNDERSTAND ITS SAFE OPERA-
     TION OR HAVE NOT READ THESE FIREARM SAFETY
     RULES OR FAIL TO AGREE TO OBEY THE RULES.

19. ALWAYS USE THE CORRECT AMMUNITION FOR YOUR
     PARTICULAR FIREARM as indicated by the marking on
     the barrel. Never use non-standard, reloaded, or "hand-
     loaded" ammunition that has not been subjected to internal
     ballistic pressure testing. Only use reloaded or non-factory
     hand-loaded ammunition after proper training and research.
     Do not use ammunition that someone gives to you without
     proper knowledge about it.

20. BEWARE OF BARREL OBSTRUCTIONS Be sure the barrel
     is clear of obstructions before shooting. Mud, water, snow, or
     other objects may inadvertently lodge in the barrel. A small
     obstruction can cause a dangerous increase in pressure inside
     the firearm and may damage your gun and cause injury to
     yourself and others when it is fired.

21. BE SURE ALL ACCESSORIES, SUCH AS HOLSTERS,
     GRIPS, SLINGS, SCOPES, AND OTHER ACCESSORIES
     ARE COMPATIBLE with the firearm and that the accesso-
     ries do not interfere with its safe operation. It is your respon-
     sibility to understand and follow all the instructions in the
     manual for your gun, well as those which may be supplied
     with your ammunition and any accessory.

22. NEVER DISASSEMBLE YOUR FIREARM beyond the sim-
     ple disassembly procedures outlined in the manual. Improper

disassembly or reassembly of your firearm may be dangerous and can lead to serious injury or death.

23. NEVER MANIPULATE, ADJUST OR CHANGE ANY OF THE INTERNAL COMPONENTS OF YOUR FIREARM UNLESS SPECIFICALLY INSTRUCTED TO DO SO IN YOUR MANUAL. Improper manipulation of any other internal component may affect the safety and reliability of your firearm and may cause serious injury or death. Never accept any advice from people on the internet. Get your information only from qualified experts recognized by manufacturers or from reliable licensed and insured gunsmiths.

24. NEVER ALLOW ANY ALTERATION OR REPLACEMENT OF PARTS IN YOUR FIREARM UNLESS PERFORMED BY A QUALIFIED GUNSMITH using genuine parts. If you do otherwise, improper functioning of your firearm may occur, and serious injury or death and property damage may result.

Those are just some of the basics when it comes to firearms handling. I would call them the 24 basic commandments of gun ownership.

There are other considerations that a person needs to know before even opening the box that their firearm comes in or transporting it home. State laws vary as to whether a firearm in the cab of your vehicle must be on your body or can be on the seat or under the seat next to you, or whether it must be locked in the trunk. You can learn the details by reading state statutes and local ordinances, or often by asking your local dealer or professional trainer.

A friend's story exemplifies just how seriously you should follow the rules of firearm safety. She grew up in a family that hunted, and she participated as a member of a target shooting team during her four years of high school. At home, she was not permitted to aim even a squirt gun at another person. She raised her sons never to point a TV remote controller at a person because it might be mistaken for a gun.

I personally saw one person who had a TV remote controller in his hand shot by police, and another person in a hallway during a search warrant who was missed by only inches when the detective mistook his TV remote controller for a gun. The police bullet hit a wall clock just behind the person. Fortunately, the person was not injured, but the detective was kidded for years for "killing time."

If you are going to get to know a firearm and its operation, then you will need to understand how to clean the firearm and keep it in top operating condition. Every time you fire a weapon, it is combusting explosive materials and releasing hot expanding gasses. Metals are being forced down the bore of the gun, scoring, and leaving deposits in the barrel. If you have ever seen a slow-motion video of a gun being fired, you can see all this material burning and coming out the barrel, the breach, and even the trigger area of the gun. That all leaves a residue that needs to be cleaned up, on both the inside and outside of the gun. Build-up can damage the weapon and can cause the firearm to malfunction, causing you or others to be injured or killed. Even if you fire a gun just once, it needs to be properly cleaned, then properly stored.

Cleaning many firearms is easy, but you need the proper tools to do it. The more complex the firearm, the more work it takes to clean it. Make sure you have read the manual and that you do not take a gun out to a range or the woods before making sure it is clean and safe. Each firearm will have specific cleaning requirements.

I am not addressing the specific details of loading and unloading and maintenance of any specific firearm in this book. They are all different from gun to gun, and you would need the correct information for the specific gun you are buying or storing.

If you have questions about any of these processes or a specific weapon, it's likely that there is a professional gunsmith in your area who can supply information, or even do assessments on the condition of a used weapon.

It is illegal to shoot at trees or use them to hold targets. These trees on public land have been shot down with fully-automatic military assault-style weapons.

CHAPTER FIFTEEN

RANGE SAFETY

The basic rules of personal firearm safety always apply, and there are a few others you will need to know if you are going to shoot at a target range. Rules for a specific indoor or outdoor range will almost always be prominently posted where everyone can see and read them. Some outdoor locations other than ranges allow recreational shooting and there will be rules for this activity. Often these will not be posted, but you must know and follow them, nonetheless. Here are some of the basic rules from the United States Forest Service for shooting on its public lands:

Target shooting is allowed on national forest or grassland unless restricted. Check your local ranger district for more information about local restrictions. It is prohibited to shoot:

1. In or within 150 yards from a residence, building, campsite, developed recreation area, or occupied area. (*Editorial Note from the Author: Personally, I think that this is nuts and it should be much further away from any of these activities or locations. Shooting near anyone camping is not only very disrespectful but will eventually get all shooting in public places banned.*)
2. Across or on a national forest or grassland road or body of water.
3. In any manner or place where any person or property is exposed to injury or damage because of such discharge.
4. Into or within a cave.
5. Firing tracer bullets or incendiary ammunition.
6. Disturbing, injuring, destroying, or in any way damaging any prehistoric, historic, or archaeological resource, structure, site, artifact, property.
7. Abandoning any personal property or failing to dispose of all garbage, including targets, paper, cans, bottles, appliances.
8. Use approved targets. Certain forests may have specific restrictions, such as the type of targets used (i.e., cardboard targets, paper targets, clay pigeons). Exploding targets are not recommended and are restricted on many forests or grasslands for safety and fire concerns. [They are also illegal in many states and actually are illegal on most other public lands]

9. Use approved targets along with a safe," bullet-proof" backstop. Do not attach your targets to vegetation or structures, such as trees, log decks, slash piles, fences, or water tanks.

10. Practice safe gun handling by:
    - Treating every gun as if it is loaded.
    - Never let the muzzle of a firearm point at anything you do not intend to shoot.
    - Keep your finger off the trigger until your sights are on the target and you are ready to shoot.
    - Make sure of your target and what is beyond.
    - Do not have alcoholic beverages while discharging a firearm."

Person with a .50 caliber sniper rifle with a scope in the forest on public land.

These are the basics, but they are only a starting place for you to do more research on your own, either with the gun manufacturer or online from reliable and reputable sources, like Federal, state, and local government websites. Stay away from blogs or other online nonsense that is often politically biased and ignores science and common-sense facts. It is unfortunate, but people can learn bad habits from seeing what other people post online on places like YouTube.

In the woods and on open rangeland, it will be up to you to abide by safety rules. If wooded or public-looking areas are not public property, but rather, are owned by private companies or individuals, I can pretty much guarantee you that all shooting on these lands is trespass and is illegal. Please do not do it. Respect private land rights. Some private owners will allow hunting, but usually ask that you get permission from them before hunting or shooting there. They'll inform you of their rules ahead of time, usually in writing and require a written permit.

Finally, try your level best to understand your moral and social responsibility to reduce conflicts with other users of forests and public lands. Be respectful, courteous, and kind when using public lands for target shooting. More of them are being closed all the time because of illegal, disrespectful, or destructive behavior. There is room for everyone if people would do more to adopt this concept. Positively interact with those who are not doing so. Try to find respectful common ground.

RPN3 Biometric Gun Safe with three opening systems.

CHAPTER SIXTEEN

FIREARM SAFETY IN YOUR HOME

Part 1 of 4 - Carrying

To get started, let's talk about keeping guns in any unsecured firearm location, including purses. Don't do it! Never leave a gun

RFID shotgun safe that bolts to the wall in a closet.

in any location that is either not on your body in a secure tamper-proof holster, in a locked safe, or at least locked with a secure trigger lock. Unfortunately, children will find handguns in their mother's purses or coat pockets and shoot someone else or themselves. It happens with unfortunate frequency. A purse or a pocket is never a safe or secure location for a firearm.

Similarly, a firearm is not safe in a briefcase or any other package or container that you are carrying and might lay down. A firearm that you carry must always be on your person and be held in a way that would make it difficult for anybody else to get it away from you. Holsters have straps and some have locking mechanisms that make guns difficult for somebody else to seize but are easy for the wearer to take out. Many police officers use these and some departments require them.

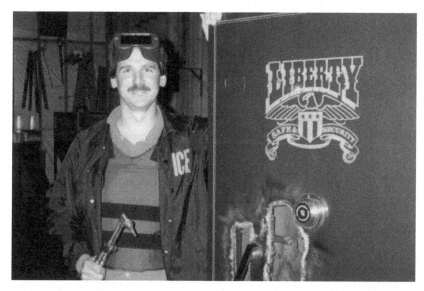

Opening a large free-standing gun safe quickly with a portable cutting torch.

If you are considering carrying a newly purchased firearm, you will need to get this security plan in place even before transporting a firearm home and make sure that everyone in your home knows the rules in advance.

Part 2 of 4– Gun Safes and Lock Boxes

One of the most important decisions you will make is how to safely store your gun at home, yet to also keep it available in case you need it to defend yourself or your family members if you are not wearing it on your person. Here are the most common choices:

Lock boxes. Firearms come from the gun shop in a simple plastic or cardboard box that is not adequate for safely storing your firearm at home. There are several ways of securing a weapon, but for starters, one of the best is a locking steel gun box. A common

Cable & key lock system for any firearm. It goes through the barrel or breech.

design for handguns is 12"x9"x4' deep, and large enough for one or two handguns. It is designed to be bolted from the inside to your floor or to the studs in the wall of your house. Some open with push buttons on top that must be depressed in a specific combination to get the box open. Manufacturers advise you to change the combination once you get the box home, using the instructions provided because the boxes come from the factory all with the same combination.

Any locked device or safe that is easy to find is a magnet to the bad guy who might burglarize your home. It says, "Hey, important and valuable things are in here!" For that reason, it's important to keep your locked firearm boxes out of sight.

Gun Safes. The size and weight of a 600-pound gun safe will prevent its being easily stolen or hauled off, but that is not your only consideration. Large upright gun safes, about the size of a small refrigerator, large enough to hold rifles and many other weapons, will keep people from getting their hands on a gun quickly, but they can be opened with some very simple tools. I can open pretty much any large free-standing gun safe in about 10 minutes or less. Many criminals, and even some amateurs or teenagers, can do this without difficulty.

Using a key to open a gun safe creates a problem in that anyone, even a child, knows how to use a key. If you use a key-operated gun safe, you will need to keep that key safely hidden where no one can find it. Your house or car key chain is not the correct place because your gun safe will be unsecure every time you lay down your keys.

A code-operated gun safe is a good option, but you need to remember the sequence of numbers you have programmed into the safe and remember them quickly if you need prompt access to the safe.

Hornady Boxes. There is another locking gun box of sorts, a wall-mounted security device that is pictured in this book. To me, it looks like a waffle iron clamped around the center of a shotgun. It is made by Hornady. You will note that it covers only part of the shotgun but keeps it from being loaded and fired when stored, while also making it available to the homeowner in less than a second. This level of security is not all that far below that of a free-standing gun safe but takes up a lot less space and could be easily hidden. It only works properly when secured into the wall behind it with tough tempered-steel bolts and nuts.

Another feature of this brand of gun-locking device is that it is controlled by a Radio Frequency Identification Device, or RFID chip. It is a small square plastic piece with electronics inside that "talks" to the gun safe, and when in proximity, pops it open. You

Expanded view of the inside of a trigger lock. It goes through the trigger of any firearm. This ones uses a key to open it.

only need to move this device close to the safe to gain access to your shotgun. It takes less than a second.

Like all security devices, this safe is only as strong as its weakest part, including where it is mounted to the wall. (Please do not think that your safety device is adequate if it is just stuck through the drywall board! This may sound insultingly simplistic, but I am aware of a painful injury that happened to a young man when exercise equipment in a commercial gym pulled out of the drywall where it had been installed with Molly bolts that did not attach the studs behind it. Like exercise equipment, gun safes need to be installed properly.)

Biometric Safes. One of the best locking systems is a biometric safe that can be opened only with the fingerprint of an authorized person, or sometimes also with a personal code that only the owner or another authorized person knows.

These work by requiring that you use your fingerprint on a small pad that you have pre-programmed into the device. You can program multiple fingerprints, usually up to 20, so you can have additional authorized people who can access the safe, or so you can use multiple fingers on your own hands in case one of your prints is too damaged or too dirty to work at any moment. Some will allow you to set a security code or use a key to open the safe as well. The code will allow access quickly, but the fingerprint is almost instant.

Although there are many options for good, secure, and quick-opening safes, I am going to feature a few companies just so you can see what they look like and how the system works for multi-opening small home gun safes. You can check many of these out online. One is called RPN3. They carry various sizes of gun safes that have all three access systems, key, biometric opening, and code. You can get the smaller ones for under $200. I am including a photo so you can see what one of them looks like. I am not endorsing that product because I have not tested it personally, but rather, I am mentioning them as a promising example of what is available.

One of the biggest arguments against the safe storage of guns is that people cannot access their weapons quickly enough in an emergency. That argument does not hold water when you see how inexpensive and easy it is to have your gun available and ready to fire in only a few moments. Many finger-imprint-type biometric locks can open in a second or less. Codes can also access the safe in a second or two. There is no way you will need a gun and be able to fire it and hit anything any quicker than that. If you are just grabbing an unsecured gun and firing it in less than that time, you are either going to shoot someone or something that should not be shot, or you are going to miss it or them entirely.

Wheel combination trigger lock on a revolver. It fits on any firearm.

Part 3 of 4 Trigger Locks

The very bare minimum of security is a good trigger lock. Because I address locks on guns or gun boxes, I should tell you that I have some professional training in working with locks. Some years ago, my police department sent me to attend the National Intelligence Academy in Fort Lauderdale, Florida. I took a series of classes on Basic and Advanced Lock Neutralization. I can get past most locks without too much difficulty. "Getting past" is the operative term. Although I can pick locks, I do what most criminals also do and just bypass the locking mechanism entirely. For example, if I wanted to steal the handgun in a locked box, I would take the whole box unless it was securely bolted to the frame of a house. Then I would just open it when I got it home with a torch, drill, or sledgehammer, at my leisure, and skip the lock. I could also reach past the locking mechanism that the key goes into and just trip the lock manually.

Where I can't bypass a locking mechanism, I can, like plenty of bad guys, make or "impression" a key to a lock almost as fast as I can pick one. This means quickly filing a new key out of a blank one by measuring the depth of the pins in the lock. Your local hardware store usually sells locks that I can impression a key for in only a couple of minutes with some very simple tools and a jeweler's loupe (the eyeglass-looking magnifying device that they wear on their heads).

Trigger locking mechanisms of several types are useful firearm safety devices for use at home, including those immobilizing the trigger, those covering the trigger entirely, and those running a cable from the breach through the muzzle and back.

Tigger guards that immobilize the trigger reach between the trigger and the trigger guard and lock the trigger so it cannot move back and fire the gun.

Trigger guards that cover the entire trigger area are made in halves that lock together from either side of the trigger guard, securely locking the trigger into place so it cannot move. Many are accessed with keys to open them back up. You may need to look at some of the photos to see how they come apart. The biggest downside of these is storing and accessing the key itself, and sometimes a downside is the quality of the lock.

Some trigger locks attach to the loops at the end of a cable that runs either through the action or up the barrel of the gun and then out the breech. This makes firearms inoperable, but only if the lock can't be easily opened, and its key is hidden. The other concern with trigger locks that go through the barrel and out of the breech is the quality of the cables. Use cables such as stainless steel that cannot be easily cut. Some new guns come with them. Some are good quality, and some are not. Inspect them carefully and note that locks made in America, not overseas, are generally much higher quality, but are also more expensive.

If you keep the key to a trigger lock with the weapon, which many people do, it becomes virtually worthless. If you cannot keep the keys separate, this system will not work, and no one will be any safer.

A significant debate is ongoing due to the poor quality of many trigger locks, especially ones given away by police departments and other organizations supporting greater security of firearms. Online news stories and posts will show trigger locks (and safes) being opened by three to six-year-olds with little difficulty. Many trigger locks can be purchased for under $4.00. A proper security device to keep a child from being killed should not be the place to save money if you are planning on being a responsible gun owner.

Since 2002, the State of California has mandated that all guns sold there must have an accompanying trigger lock or locking device, but the device also must be approved by the state's Department of Justice Bureau of Firearms. You can access their safety recommendations and locking requirements here: https://oag.ca.gov/firearms This law came into place due to the poor-quality of devices that are either sold or given away.

I would also warn you against getting what is known as "disc tumbler locks," like the ones on common filing cabinets. I can open these in no more than 2 seconds with nothing more than a paperclip. You can probably do it in less than 30 seconds without any of the training that I have had. Teenagers and even younger kids will figure them out just as quickly.

Disc tumbler locks are easy to identify if you look inside where the key goes in. There are no pins, but just a series of flat discs that slip up and down on springs. Millions of these have been made and distributed by well-meaning people and groups in efforts to get people to secure their guns. I do not believe that they are safe because they are far too easy to open by anyone using minimal effort.

Fingerprint biometric trigger lock that can go on any firearm. The fingerprint reader is on the side. This has a high level of safety.

Trigger locks are safer if their locks have pin tumblers with at least four or five pins. Even better is a lock that has at least one "mushroom" pin, if you can find one. A single mushroom pin will make the lock almost unpickable. Many of them permanently jam when you try to pick them, so they can never be opened again after someone has tried to open them without a key. This internal self-destruct mechanism makes them among the more secure locks that exist for any purpose. Makers of good locks will heavily advertise their safety features on the packages they are sold in.

For a little more money, you can get a biometric trigger lock. This dispenses with the key, but unlike the biometric gun safe that has multiple opening mechanisms, these are usually single system opening devices. Biometric locks, although probably the most secure, also need to have a functioning power source (usually a battery or two) inside of them, and it must be a battery that has not died. They are very good and more secure, but they need to be maintained, which a keyed lock does not. A good quality one costs in the range of $200.

Combination locks with little wheels and numbers on top are not a great idea. These are the ones that you see on briefcases. Once the notches on the inside edge of the wheels, which look like little gears, are all lined up, which only takes a few moments with a magnifying glass, you just rotate the numbers on the top together all at once, and the lock pops open. The key to identifying these poor-quality locks is to look at the space between the wheels with the numbers on the top that spin, and the metal on the sides of them. To be safe, they need to be so tight in that space that you can't see between them, even with a magnifying glass, or be able to get even a thin piece of paper down along the side. If the wheels with the numbers seem loose or wobbly, it is a worthless lock. They should fit snug and feel almost tight when you advance the wheels with the numbers.

Lower security or cheap locking mechanisms can be opened by just reaching to the back of the lock and pulling the lock open, completely bypassing the entire locking system itself. This means that the actual mechanism that holds the lock closed is at the back of the lock and it is not covered by a plate. You simply put something small into the lock and pull it open. That takes less than one second.

Part 4 of 4 - A Crime Proof Gun - Full Biometric Firearms

I want you to know about the newest and potentially most secure gun in the world. You understand the concept now of biometrics on safe gun storage; now think about a gun that has such a device built right into it.

You may recall that one of the biggest dangers of owning, displaying, or pointing a gun at someone is that often the bad guy will take it from you and shoot you with it. But what if someone took your gun, and as soon as it left your hand, it locked up inside and could not be fire? What about a gun that could not fire a bullet by any unauthorized person in your home, or by any person besides you for that matter?

These types of firearms are real, and more progress is being made on them every day. They are commonly called "smart guns." They use two different types of technology. One is the biometric system requiring your fingerprint to be wrapped around the gun handle or stock for the gun to be activated. Without your fingerprint, the weapon will be mechanically locked from the inside, and it cannot fire. In the past, consumers have complained that these operated too slowly. Their other problem has been with the fingerprint readers themselves. But as technology improves, so have these reading devices. The current ones are far more reliable. I think that as this technology progresses, smart firearms will become the standard of the industry and that someday a gun without this type of device will only be found in a museum.

The second type of "smart gun" uses a very different type of technology called RFID, or radio frequency identification device, like in the Hornady gun safe listed above. The firearm is locked from the inside until it gets into the proximity of a ring or wristwatch that you are wearing. The gun and your ring or watch quickly communicate and the gun lock comes off inside the weapon automatically. This is like a key card in a hotel or your office building. The ring or watch must be within five to ten inches for them to connect, just like a key card on a door. This way, if you drop the gun, or it is taken away from you, it immediately locks up and cannot fire. It is highly unlikely that a person would know that you had this device, or where exactly where it was located, although hiding the unlocking device will become more important if RFID weapons become more familiar to the general population.

These RFID and biometric guns are not widely available in America just yet. One of the problems is that early models from American manufacturing companies misread fingerprints one out of a hundred times. This made these early versions a non-starter for police departments that could not allow that rate of malfunction.

The concept of smart guns also become political. People on the right expressed anger that this technology was being developed at all, for fear this technology would lead to the banning and seizure of all guns without it. Gun rights advocates stopped buying guns from any American company that was even considering or working on this technology. People on the left and in the technology industry itself did not want to make anything that helped more people acquire guns, no matter how safe they were. They were both wrong.

Wherever there is a market, entrepreneurs will emerge to provide any product that people will buy. This marketplace will be evolving in new ways after January 6, 2021. Any gunmaker who isn't offering these soon will be on the outside looking in on a very lucrative market. Some European companies are perfecting this technology right now and are continuing where their American counterparts left off only a few years ago.

One American company developing these biometric firearms is called Biofire. They launched a new website in 2021. Although I am not endorsing or recommending their specific product because I have not personally tested it yet, you can read more about the firm online and even be put on a list for when their products become available. As a consumer, you can influence the marketplace of the future by showing your support for these smarter products over less-safe firearms.

No new safety technology is ever perfect at first, but a long time ago people said the same thing about seat belts, and later, airbags in cars. Today, we would not think of driving a car without both. In the not-too-distant future, every car in the world will have a backup camera, just so we don't run over little kids on bikes and pedestrians. The same will be true of technology for smart guns.

CHAPTER SEVENTEEN

NEGLIGENCE & THE VERY END OF YOUR LIFE

In South Carolina on Christmas day in December 2021, at 2:30 in the afternoon, the Henderson County Sheriff's Office responded to a terrible and completely preventable call for help. When emergency workers arrived, they found that a 3-year-old girl had suffered a gunshot wound. She had accessed an unsecured firearm and shot herself, but was still clinging to life. This is by far one of the worst calls any police officer or medic can respond to. No matter how experienced or battle-hardened someone is, this is one of the calls that rips your heart out.

Due to the devastating injuries, the child was airlifted to nearby Mission Hospital and went into surgery. The heroic aid workers and doctors did everything they could to save her life. Medical staff is also deeply impacted by these senseless injuries to small children. After over 72 agonizing hours for this shocked community, police officers, medical workers, and family, the small child died of her terrible wounds. This will be a Christmas to remember for everyone involved, but in the most devastating way possible.

Although this has been covered in some other chapters, I want to emphasize it once again. It's that important. Just like alcohol and guns are a toxic match, so are kids and guns. Before buying, training with, transporting, or owning a gun, you need to think this over. If a child gets their hands on your gun, something virtually unimaginable up to this point in your life will very possibly happen. Your life will never be the same again. You can forget all your dreams and plans, or any semblance of normal life after that point in time. You will think of it every minute of every day until you die. It is an image that will never leave your mind. This will be a life-ending event that could happen to you.

Besides the horror you would feel, you could also have significant liability, criminal in many states, and civil liability in any state if you did not secure your firearm and it was used to harm someone else.

Improperly stored or mishandled firearms are responsible for killing or wounding 18,000 kids from the ages of 1 to 19 years old in America each year. Guns are the leading cause of death for this age group. Of that above number, over 5,100 are aged 17 and younger, so it isn't just young adults. There do not need to be any such incidents or accidents.

Although you cannot control what other people do, you can make sure that you are not going to be a part of this problem or statistic. If you have decided to get a firearm, then you need to review all the safety advice you have read in this book. Make a list and think it over. Use it as a checklist. It is not all that difficult, but you need to have a safety plan and you need to keep to it.

CHAPTER EIGHTEEN

ADVANCED TRAINING

If you decide to train with a firearm, there are topics beyond safety to think about. The first step is easy: Orientation, safety, firing at targets, and cleaning a gun are not difficult. There are classes and instructors who are good at this basic work, no matter where you live. Firearm safety and basic hunting classes are excellent places to meet interesting people who are there to help you, usually without a political agenda. Some courses are done outdoors, some at indoor ranges. Some states sponsor gun safety classes.

Once you have learned the basics of firing your weapon and maintaining it, you may wish to move on to practical uses in tactical situations. This is very different. Targets do not shoot back at you. If you need to shoot someone, he or she will not just hold still while you do it. You can experience mental and emotional processes that, if not properly prepared for, make virtually everything you know about using a firearm worthless. The first time you must use a firearm in a tactical situation, you will not be ready if target shooting is all you have done.

When I started my police career in Washington State, all officers at the Basic Academy were sent to the Seattle Police Academy
shooting range in South Seattle. The instructors were professionals, and the facility was well run and safe. The officers who worked
there were assigned to just this one job. They could teach you to
hit the target and handle your firearm safely. If you could not pass
their standards during this training, you would flunk out of your
career in police work and could not work as a commissioned officer anywhere in Washington State. The class on shooting took 40
hours.

Later, police departments realized that being able to hit a paper
target had little do to with being able to handle a tactical situation.
When stress was significant, that original training often flew right
out the window. Ongoing training was ordered, and competency
was required to be renewed on an ongoing basis with in-service
training.

We who were being retrained hated it at first because it was a
lot of work and it made us sweat, but eventually we began to see it
as being critically important. At a range, we had to exert ourselves
by both running and shooting in the same exercise. We would do
some shooting, and then had to run until our pulses shot up, then
stood or lay down and fired at the targets while our hearts were
pounding. That replicated our responses to shooting situations. It
required a great deal of discipline to be accurate while shooting,
reloading quickly, and then beginning to shoot again at multiple
targets.

That is how you will feel the first time someone points a gun or
is firing at you. Through training or experience, you can become
more accustomed to it, and you may respond quite differently and
be a bit calmer, but the first time will always be stressful.

The next step in advanced training was to address instant
decision-making while under extreme stress. Police departments

were moving beyond basic weapons proficiency. It was not that difficult to simulate the body's response to stress manually with heavy physical exertion, but this did not force other critical thinking functions to be tested as well. What evolved was called "Shoot, don't shoot" training. It was clever: Added to facing strict time limits and physical exertion to replicate stress, we had targets pop up unannounced. We would have no idea whether these instant threats were good guys or bad guys. We couldn't just shoot any target that popped up. The target might represent a child running away from a kidnapper. Other targets posed lethal threats that justified our shooting them. Sometimes the line between shooting or not was very thin. We had only a moment to make these decisions. Errors in judgment and thinking were not acceptable.

Then police training moved to its ultimate level to date. It was called "mock scenes." In Washington State, the trainers created an entire indoor location called "Mock City." Trainees could go on "patrol" in this made-up city that had realistic buildings and related props. It had academy staff as actors posing in situations that the trainee did not know were coming. This replication of the real world, in which trainees had to face realistic life and death situations and decisions, became excellent training.

The point of this training was for officers to feel like they were facing a genuine unannounced tactical threat. It wasn't just firearms training that was being tested; it also tested the mental functioning necessary to take a life, or not, in these situations. The real benefit lay in officers' thinking through scenarios in advance. That was well over half the battle. A trainee who could understand how to process and solve problems in realistic and stressful situations was well on the way to accessing that same critical thinking when it came time to use that skill on the job. Killing another person is something that is difficult for any sane person to do. But this is a door to a place in the brain that, once found and opened, can be opened again when the need arises.

With shoot/don't shoot and mock situations, outcomes improved. The objective of preventing unnecessary police shootings was met with this training, along with quicker decision-making in the necessary deployment of deadly force.

If you want to become proficient at defense with a firearm, then you can find and attend similar training courses yourself, and you will understand what it will be like if you must fire at another person. You will either find this skill, or possibly find that you are incapable of ever doing it. Either way, you will be a safer and more responsible gun owner. Your objective is to learn to beat people in combat who have no such training or personal experience, and good instructors can address your individual questions and concerns.

In my estimation, you don't get points for second place in a gunfight. If you are going to be a gun owner, then you need to be a responsible, trained, and informed one, or don't be one at all. We have far too many of the bad kind already.

Illegal, toxic and exploding targets from USFS lands.

CHAPTER NINETEEN

FIRING WILD – GUNS IN THE FOREST

A s you make your plan to acquire and train with your firearm, you may be tempted to skip the range and go right to the

woods to fire your gun. Please do not do that. Heading right out
to the woods to begin banging away is like going to medical school
right after kindergarten. Looking for public places to shoot should
only come after competent firearms training from an instructor.

There may be a place for you to do some shooting or training later once you are properly acquainted with your firearm. The
basic range safety rules and all those standards also apply to the
woods or public lands. Public lands will also have individual local
standards and rules about where you can shoot and what you can
shoot into or around.

If you go open shooting in these places, consider this: Many
areas are being destroyed by irresponsible shooters. This is unfortunate because done properly, target shooting can be a compatible
use of public lands. The explosion of gun sales in the last 10 years
has led to a staggering misuse of our public lands by unintelligent,
drunk, unsafe, and uninformed gun owners. Millions of dollars of
damage in the form of wildfires and pollution have been caused in
Washington State by illegal and unsafe target shooting.

I live close to one of those areas near a national forest and
see it all the time. One shooting area that is now closed saw eight
wildfires in a single summer from users shooting illegal explosive
targets. One happened in August when the temperature was 87
degrees with only 17% humidity, making fire danger very high.
Citizens in my area formed a group to inform shooters, clean up
the mess, and get some dangerous places closed. The Washington
State legislative staff made a public video that shows what it looks
like in the forests when these nitwits come up with their weapons.
I would suggest you look at it now. It can be found here on You-
Tube – it's called Firing Wild:

https://www.youtube.com/watch?v=sNMBCQowVjM

The totally stupid stuff you will see here was posted by the idiots themselves online. You can't make this stuff up. I want you to remember two things. The first is that these people know nothing about firearms or firearm safety. You need to watch out for and stay away from them in the woods. The second is another point that I am trying to make in this book about the actual danger from most Americans with firearms today. You will note the complete lack of discipline and thought that many have put into owning firearms. These are not tactically disciplined people. Some are not even very bright. Many such American gun owners pose just as great a risk to themselves as to others.

Some of the idiots using these areas were bringing up cars, cranking the steering wheels into a turn with the seatbelt, putting a brick on the accelerator, and then jumping out. The car would spin wildly out of control in circles at high speed with no one in it. They would then blast away with their AR-15 type weapons until the car would explode into flames; they'd keep shooting until the car finally stopped with thousands of bullets and holes in it. Shooting cars, electronics, and huge TVs leaves toxic chemicals.

Another subject to think about when target training in the woods, or on any public lands that are open to shooting, is the dual problem of toxic chemicals and lead. Each causes a toxic risk.

Stupid people with guns learn which chemicals make the biggest fireballs and bring those materials up to the woods. Unfortunately, many of these chemicals that look so cool when they blow up are also carcinogenic, and the heavy metals in them are persistent in the environment.

One area near where I live had so much shooting of toxic chemicals that we hired a lab to analyze the soil. It showed that there were significant levels of dangerous toxic chemicals that could contaminate a person just by walking in the area. We presented

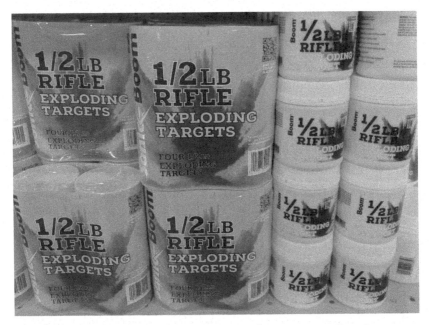

Exploding targets like this Tanerite by Sonic Boom are illegal on most public lands and start forest fires.

the results to the USFS, and the area was closed to shooting and capped and sealed with a deep overlay of gravel, at significant expense to the taxpayers.

The second problem was the levels of lead in this area. One area had lead levels that were 1,800 times above what is considered toxic in a workplace environment. It would have qualified as a superfund site.

If you go to shoot in the woods, you can expect that if the area has been used for some time, lead levels might be this high. No one cleans up the lead like they often do at a shooting range where they have a safety feature called lead traps. This does not mean that you cannot shoot there, but you need to know that your shoes can be contaminated until you clean them. If I am walking in these areas, I use a separate set of shoes that I keep in a sealed package in the trunk of my car. I slip them on and off from the driver's seat from a short distance away from the firing range, and then put a plastic garbage bag on the floor of my car to keep my car uncontaminated. When I change back into my clean shoes, I drop the dirty shoes into the contaminated bag without touching the outside, keeping my trunk clean.

You should never eat or drink anything in an active shooting area like this, or any other location for that matter, where guns have been fired. This is a warning that most gun manufacturers will advise you of when you purchase a firearm. You should never touch your mouth or face after shooting, handling a gun, or even being in this type of area, because you can ingest lead. Enough lead in your system, or more seriously, in the system of a younger person, can cause cancer and brain damage. Hostility, agitation, anger, paranoia, and insanity can be the result of ingesting lead.

You will also see a lot of people with military-assault style weapons in the woods. The reason is that many ranges don't allow them to be shot on their property. Additionally, there is no range master on public lands to control their behavior like there is on most gun ranges. You need to keep an eye out for these people and keep your distance. Many are abjectly unsafe in basic firearms handling.

The good news is that you can help prevent all of this from happening. You can also help protect our public lands from irresponsible shooters by reporting bad actors. Although it may not be your cup of tea, if I see someone shooting illegally, I ask them to stop. They are usually only doing it because no one ever asks them to stop, and in some cases, they do not know the rules. I will tell them where they can shoot legally and what legal and safe targets are. The vast majority are polite and not confrontational. Some thank me for the information.

When it comes to protecting our public lands, we are all in this together. In my area, our group has reduced illegal and unsafe target shooting and trash substantially in the last six years. Our group is called the White River Forest Protection Association, and we have shooters and non-shooters alike among our members.

August 12, 2017. White supremacists gather for the Unite the Right rally in Charlottesville, Virginia, Sean Rayford, Alamy Photo.

CHAPTER TWENTY

FASCISM & NAZIS

These days people use two terms a lot, "fascism," and "Nazis," but many do not even know what they mean. Fascism is a far-right ultranationalism dictatorship, suppression of opposition and regimentation of society, and it is dangerous. Nazism was the dogma of the Nationalist Socialist German Workers Party under

Hitler during the 1930s and 1940s, and today means extremely racist and authoritarian behavior. Some people use these terms anytime a law is passed, or executive orders are issued, that they do not like. They call it fascism. On the contrary, even though you hear it frequently, Americans are still free to vote for their government, their votes are counted, and all three branches of our government are functioning. People can contest any law or order they do not like in the courts. Any contested law or order found to violate the constitution is nullified. There is no fascism today in America. No one person can declare any law or order unconstitutional themselves, or just by saying that it is. That is anarchy. We govern ourselves collectively and that is democracy. It does a great disservice, demeaning the work of the men and women who have fought for our nation against real fascists and Nazis, to complain that any law one dislikes is "fascism."

Fascism takes power away from the other branches of government and consolidates it in the dictatorship. Fascism's first step is to overturn free and fair elections and eventually to end voting altogether.

Since the coup attempt on our capitol on January 6, 2021, America's confidence in the strength of our country has been shaken. By the end of 2021, a plurality of all Americans believed that we were headed towards a second Civil War. Over 60% of Americans are at least very worried about it. Most people are just worried. But many partisan supporters of Trumpism welcome a second Civil War and see it as a good, if not a necessary development, to help bring a Trumpian dictatorship to America.

Folks who are buying weapons and ammunition to help usher in a fascist Trumpian dictatorship have been stockpiling weapons and bullets for years. I happen to live in a rural area and see such militants practicing in the national forests with their military-style assault weapons, both fully and semi-automatic. Sometimes they are dressed in uniforms and full combat tactical gear. It is very common to see Trump symbols and anti-Jewish Nazi symbols side by side with many of these folks. The Southern Poverty Law Center, an institution that works for civil rights and which tracks hate groups, documents these groups and their dramatic increase in the era of Trump and deems them to be dangerous.

Although we also have some members of the insurrectionist organizations Proud Boys and Oath Keepers in this part of the country, one local group that is predominately anti-Jewish and anti-Black is the "Atomwaffen Division" and I have seen them many times in the forests in their signature uniforms and qua-si-tactical gear. They wear pro-Hitler messages and Swastikas. Members are notable for the skull face masks they wear to hide their identities when they are out shooting. These self-described Nazi idealists often wear masks to hide their identities, but then some post undisguised pictures and videos of themselves on the internet! They can't help it.

Usually, they just blast away and don't seem to understand anything about real tactical training with their weapons. Any person with police or military training would laugh at their "training" sessions in the woods.

Several of the members of the "Atomwaffen Division" are now in Federal prison or are awaiting their trials and or sentences for their overtly terrorist activities. They have been involved in weapons violations, drug dealing, and threats to transportation and power systems. They have also publicly posted anti-Semitic posters and threatened journalists in the Seattle area who were reporting on them. One local reporter that was specifically threatened after investigating them was Chris Ingalls of KING-5 News. He has given interviews that you can find online about how these types of threats affected him. Their downfall? An FBI informant. More about that in Chapter 23 called, "Snitches Get Stitches". The leader of the Oath Keepers, Elmer Stewart Rhodes III has been charged with seditious conspiracy, and Henry "Enrique" Tarrio of the Proud Boys has also been indicted for their organizations' actions on January 6th of 2021.

The groups named by the Southern Poverty Law Center, although dangerous, are not necessarily the worst ones we should be most afraid of. It is the ones we don't hear about that pose a greater risk. There are people arming themselves who adhere to Trumpism and keep to themselves. They are cautious of others finding out about their activities and plans. Often, they are heavily armed, and in some cases, better trained in the use and handling of more complex military weapons. They are not a majority of the run-of-the-mill far-right gun owners, but they are a sizable group. I have come across many of them in the forests. They tend to know what they are doing with military-style weapons and have at least a rudimentary level of tactical training. A sign of them is often a large swastika on the neck, or information on them or their vehicles indicating adherence to the QAnon beliefs, usually in a code not meant to be understood by outsiders. Sometimes more overt statements of these beliefs come from people like Republican Congresswoman Marjorie Taylor-Green from Georgia, who also said that California forest fires had been started by blue Jewish lasers from outer space, but many others are more secretive.

There is a misperception that the disloyal insurrectionists of January 6, 2021, were predominately former military combat veterans. That is nonsense. The insurrectionists were primarily people who dressed up and posed as combat veterans. Loyal American combat veterans do not support such activities. Veterans of actual combat are also only a small percentage of retired or former military personnel as a whole. Their number may be as small as two or three percent, depending on the branch of service. Many people pretend to be combat veterans when they are not.

The real problem for our society is that no matter whether they are trained or not, some people are getting ready for this second Civil War as best they can. They plan to do anything Trump tells them to do to help him overthrow our democratic republic. In sheer numbers, they create a problem, just like Hitler's "Brown Shirts" of the 1930s in Germany.

Democracies may be more fragile than we had thought. If Trump is gone, Florida Governor Ron DeSantis has made it clear that he is ready and willing to step in to fill Trump's shoes. In early 2022, there were violent Nazi protests in his state that all rational and civilized leaders of both parties immediately condemned. DeSantis was silent for two days. Finally, when the pressure to address this shocking development became too much, he said that he was the victim himself and he attacked those pointing out his failure to condemn the anti-Semitic Nazi rallies and beliefs. The end of Trump will not signal the end of the fascist movement in America. Several prominent senators and governors are all jockeying positions to take this mantle and go forward, should Trump fall out of favor. Some may end up being far more dangerous than Trump.

Don't underestimate right-wing movements these days. Prior to WWII, people didn't think Hitler would accomplish much of anything because they all knew he was an unintelligent, verbose, but well-spoken nut case. Even in Germany, he was seen as a fool and almost entirely out of touch with political, social, and economic reality. People on the streets would joke about him. They became accustomed to his nasty speeches and constant insults to anyone who disagreed with him. He never debated anything or anyone, he just attacked others with bombastic and utterly crazy and untrue statements and lies. His supporters ate it up and most regular people just laughed it off. Nothing was done to prepare for what was coming.

Hitler went on to try to fulfill his promise to restore Germany to its pre-WWI strength, but he ended up destroying much of

Europe, causing the deaths of 60 million people. Then it was too late to start getting prepared.

If they had known all of this was going to happen, Germans would have had weapons in advance and the response would have been immediate and impactful. The Nazis might never have gotten much of a foothold in many occupied areas. They might never have gotten into power in Germany in the first place.

Hitler's Brownshirts were mostly just bullies when together with others. They got their way and intimidated voters, mostly just by threatening and carrying weapons that they seldom actually used beyond roughing people up. Once Hitler got 44% of the vote, he became Chancellor and got rid of the legislative branch of the German government. He and his supporters ended elections altogether.

Some Americans buying and "training" with their weapons are doing so today for similar purposes. It is a show of force that they are primarily working on. They feel that if they have enough guns, their opponents who see them will capitulate.

If enough people who support our democratic republic acquire and train with enough weapons, this all becomes much less likely. The primary force to fight such a war is each state's National Guard, but ordinary citizens may have to do so and become the "resistance."

The concept here is making sure that a dictator never gets to consolidate power. An informed, determined, and properly armed population can keep that from happening. What liberals, Democrats, and others need to ask is, are you okay with just Trump-type supporters getting and keeping all the guns and ammunition? What could happen if you don't give it some thought? Safe and proper gun ownership by citizens concerned for our democratic republic can pose a significant deterrent to a dictator taking power here in the first place. Trump-type supporters are banking on your failing to consider this.

CHAPTER TWENTY-ONE

WHAT TO HIDE AND WHERE TO HIDE IT

Part 1 of 2 – Locations to Hide Weapons and Ammunition

If you are storing a firearm for some future militia or resistance purpose and are not going to open the box and fire it yourself, keep the original manual and any spare parts or cleaning kits with it, then make sure the storage container for your weapon is completely watertight and closed to all outside elements for long-term storage. That can be the end of your firearms training and preparation to be in the "resistance."

When I say "secure" I mean very secure. Large free-standing gun safes are not for this purpose. Everyone knows that gun safes hold guns. In the case of a dictatorship taking control of our country and its supporters coming to your house, a gun safe would be a sure sign that you not only had a gun, but where you'd stored it.

The best place for a weapon for future use is locked up and hidden somewhere that no one can get into, or even find in the first place. You would never want this type of weapon to get into the hands of anyone outside of its intended purpose. It would be best if no one even knew you had it. You would also not want it to be found in your house if it were searched by a dictatorial regime.

Many of the weapons for the resistance hidden in WWII were buried in the ground. Some were built into walls in houses and were almost impossible to find. Those hidden improperly were discovered in searches and their owners were often imprisoned or killed by the regime. Hiding something in your house so it cannot be found takes some work and thought.

One fairly simple way to hide a firearm is to open an existing wall and put the weapon and rounds of ammunition in with it, and then seal the wall back up with drywall or whatever so it looks like it did before the work began. The weapon would never be available for use without some difficulty and work. If this were done in areas where there are metal pipes or other types of structural metals in the building, the weapon would also not be detectible by a magnet or metal detector. Other surrounding metal can disguise the shape of a gun, even from X-rays. Inside or under cabinets can also be good hiding places once closed back up. This does not mean just putting them on the shelves, but having them built into areas that do not open for usual access and storage.

One of the best hiding places I ever saw was uncovered during a search warrant and concealed 15 ounces of contraband cocaine built into a pinball machine. We knew the drugs were in the house but could not find them. After hours of searching, we brought in a drug-sniffing dog named "Pounder" who was operated by a Seattle police officer. Within 10 minutes, Pounder sat at the front of the pinball machine, and sure enough, we found the cocaine. We would have never found it without the help of the drug dog.

Even when drugs are packaged carefully, they still give off an odor that dogs can detect. Guns are a lot harder to find because

Model 66 S&W .357 Combat Magnum w_4.25″ barrel.

most dogs can't detect them. Properly cleaned guns with no odor of burnt powder or residue are very difficult to detect.

Part 2 of 2 - What to Hide - Packaging & Materials

If you are hiding a weapon, remember that it is useless without ammunition. I would suggest that 200 to 500 rounds are the minimum of what you might think of hiding along with the weapon, possibly divided into a couple of different locations, just in case one parcel is found. These items need to be put into plastic bags and sealed from the elements, like heat, cold, moisture and vermin.

Removing all the ambient air from the gun and ammo packages is important. You can push or suck the air out once the plastic is sealed or use a leaf blower by plugging it into the sucking function. Food bag sealers that remove all the air are also great for this when packaging ammunition.

A few other items like a small brush that goes on a long aluminum shaft to clean the inside of the barrel are also necessary. There will be a cleaning kit available for virtually any firearm when you purchase it. A broken or improperly maintained firearm will be unreliable and it could become inaccurate, so I would place the owner's manual in plastic packaging and hide it as well. I would not keep the manual where it could be found, because it is a strong indication that there are firearms hidden in the house.

Burying and hiding weapons in the ground is an option, but you must take great care that the packaging is entirely sealed against the elements. I'd start with a hard-locking plastic gun or metal case with an eggshell foam barrier inside, completely seal all edges of the outer gun case with epoxy, and then a layer of silicone sealant, then package it in several successive layers of heavy plastic, also vacuum sealed.

There are three different types of weapons that might be useful for future resistance situations. One is a long rifle that can shoot people from significant distances away. You might think of this as a sniper type of situation. Resistance organizations used these frequently against Nazis in WWII. Unfortunately, they often had to adapt and shoot old WWI military weapons that were not ideal. The bullets were very large and powerful, but also traveled slowly and were brought down by gravity too quickly. Sometimes the barrels were "shot out", meaning that the rifling was so worn that the weapons were inaccurate.

Another concept affecting your choice is that a rifle needs to be extremely simple. There is nothing simpler and more reliable than a bolt action rifles. They can hold several rounds and fire one each time you use the "bolt" to eject a round and push another into the firing chamber. They will work in any condition or weather. They virtually never jam or fail to fire, unlike semi or fully automatic weapons that can be notoriously unreliable over time. The only limitation is that the weapon's scope must work properly and be on target.

This type of weapon will generally use a single shot to neutralize the target. After that, the person using it will be leaving the area as quickly as possible. That is how they were used in real-life situation in WWII in countries that were occupied by the Nazis.

To be accurate, a rifle needs a scope. There are two styles to consider. One is a variable distance scope with an eyepiece that you can twist to see different distances. Many times, this is the best, as you may not know ahead of time the distance you will be shooting for which you need an accurate image. However, extra moving parts can malfunction. The more complex the mechanism is, the more chances it has for something to go wrong or break. The alternative is a fixed distance scope that only magnifies at a single distance. Everything at any distance is clear, but you cannot "zoom" in.

The most reliable hunting scopes in the world are generally 4x scopes (4x means zoomed in 4 times closer) but they are not quite as good at longer distances. There are other fixed magnification scopes, but most today are variable. Their quality and reliability are often directly proportional to their price.

Regarding the numbers on scopes, in a 3-9x40 scope, the 3 means three power, or 3x. This means that the image you see through the scope appears three times (3x) closer than it does with your naked eye. With a fixed 4x, or 4 power scope, the image is four times closer, and you cannot change it or zoom in.

The 9x variable means nine power, or nine times (9x) closer than it appears with your naked eye. The forty (40) is the size of the diameter of the objective lens (at the front, far end of the scope from your eye) measured in millimeters. With a variable scope like this, you can dial in the distance you want to magnify.

I happen to like Redfield Scopes, the ones that are made in the US. The 4x power wide-field fixed is one of my favorites. I can hit something reliably at 200 yards all day long with this scope without any difficulty. It never drifts off target. It is a very simple design and is ruggedly built.

Leupold scopes made in the U.S. are also high quality and reasonably priced. A 3-9x40 would be an excellent sniper scope, but again, they have more moving parts and will take more maintenance. The best option is to have two scopes, both a fixed 4x scope and a 9x variable one as well. With two, you have a backup if one does malfunction, and they can work in different situations.

A rifle with a scope cannot hit anything until the whole thing is "sighted in," which means that the scope is adjusted with some screws so the image in the middle of the crosshairs in the scope is where the bullet hits. A person who is using the rifle is going to want to test the rifle and sight it in before using it. It might be best to buy a good scope and store it in its original box and hide it away.

No scope will work without the proper scope mounts that hold the scope onto the weapon. Make sure you have at least one, or even two of these, and that they will fit the weapon and scope(s) that you have bought. Also, make sure that you have any required tools or materials used to attach the scope to the rifle. They will be explained in the instructions. Once properly fitted, some can be left on, and others can come off and go back on with ease and no tools at all.

Earlier we talked about different types of handguns, both small and concealable, and ones for tactical operations and shooting at close range at normal handgun distance of several feet to up to 50 feet. Good quality handguns are reliable and do not need work, just cleaning, to keep them firing. Package them in the original containers and seal them. If you are going to this much trouble, do not bother with older, used, worn, or handguns unless you know they are in excellent working condition.

You might ask about getting and storing an AR-15 or similar weapon. As you now know, these are primarily offensive weapons as opposed to being good defensive ones. As such, they can be useful in warfare situations. Even a small number of them in the hands of skillful operators can be used to attack a group of people and be very successful. The Dutch underground would have loved a few of these for killing gatherings of Nazis during WWII. If you are just storing one, there is a good chance someone with training and experience can use it. If you personally do not have the proper training and experience, then don't plan on getting much of that experience and training after everything has gone wrong. If you happen to be wealthy, you could buy a number of these and store them, but I would not put them all in the same location. Weapons and ammunition stored all in one place was a mistake that was made in WWII-occupied areas.

A shogun such as a Mossberg 12-gauge Marine Corps stainless steel, or the more modern Mossberg 590A1 Tactical, would be both a devastatingly powerful defensive and offensive tactical weapon to store. In the right hands, there is nothing to match it at 50 yards or less. In war, collateral damage is far less of an issue than using it against a shooter in a school or shopping mall today. At close combat distances, I would take one of these over a dozen AR-15s any day of the week. Get one and secure it.

You will probably want to know where to buy these firearms. Many larger chain outdoor stores no longer sell any type of military-style assault weapons. I also believe that there is a moral component to this type of purchase. Most competent and professional gun dealers do not wish to become political or arm the wrong types of people illegally. But not all of them. Check out the reputation of your local gun stores.

Many "Gun Shows" have been notoriously lax about putting weapons into the hands of anyone who wanted them, including criminals and mentally ill people, without doing background checks. I would not spend my money there.

You can ship rifles, but not handguns by USPS. FedEx and UPS can ship them, but only to people with federal firearms licenses. Most gun stores have this designation.

Again, the hope is that these hidden weapons and ammunition would never be necessary to use in America, and if you had suggested this as a good idea to me in 2014, I would have thought you were certifiably nuts. But not anymore. Most people I know today understand that the risk of a dictatorship taking over America is no longer an entirely fantastical delusion and that Trump is not the only person who might lead people to such an end.

CHAPTER TWENTY-TWO

FIGHT CLUB FOR DEMOCRATS

W hat is the first rule of "Fight Club"? If you've seen the movie, of course, you know that the first rule of Fight Club is that you never talk about Fight Club. The second rule about Fight Club? You never talk about Fight Club. This 1999 movie with Bran Pitt and Edward Norton is a great classic movie, but I remind you of it here because of the concept: When you purchase a firearm, whether, for yourself or others, you don't talk about it.

I am a big fan of Brad Pitt and some of the movies he has made about fighting and killing Nazis, like "Inglorious Bastards" or "Fury" and I enjoy his ideas of bringing Nazis to justice in various and creative ways. I really like the scene where WWII is ended early by one of the Nazis making a deal to help kill Hitler and his entire staff at a movie theater in occupied France. In truth, many German Army leaders attempted to assassinate Hitler, but they failed in all these plots. One of the most famous involved Lieutenant Colonel Claus von Stauffenberg on July 20, 1944, near

Raustenburg in East Prussia. This group of conspirators is a good example of how people must operate in such cases. Their plan worked in blowing up the building that Hitler was in, but Hitler survived. The conspirators were, however, able to carry it out without being detected. Secrecy was their ally.

The first thing any dictator will do after taking over America will be to take away everyone's guns. Dictators always need to control all the guns themselves. If this happens, and anyone knows you have a gun, everyone else will know very quickly. You will lose it. Your plan will be worthless.

If your point is to have a gun for the protection or restoration of our American democratic republic, then you should not be telling anyone about it. Procure it and store it in a way that people do not know anything about it. It should be something that you eventually even forget about yourself over time until such an event takes place. It will be invaluable for such a purpose if properly hidden.

There was an excellent book published in 2021 called *Three Ordinary Girls: The Remarkable Story of Three Dutch Teenagers Who Became Spies, Saboteurs, Nazi Assassins-and WWII Heroes*, by Tim Brady. If you think you might face a situation such as a threat to American democracy, you might wish to read this book. It points out the dangers of people knowing the identities and resources of the resistance under the regime of a tyrannical dictatorship like Hitler's. The same thing happened in most other occupied countries in WWII. Although the allies did their best to free the world of nationalism and radical racism during WWII, the people themselves had to do more than just wait for years to be rescued. Brave people, like these teenage girls and many others, heeded the call to action. How the girls hardened and adapted to their situations is well explained. If even 1,000 Dutch people had made these types of secret preparations in advance and had stored modern and operable weapons, they might have collapsed the Nazi regime in a matter of months, not years.

This is not to say that if such an event happens, you will be the person, like these girls, who will be doing the direct fighting to restore democracy and civilized order. Not a lot of people did. These types of operations are not for everyone. But the ones who did were helped by scores of others in supporting roles who supplied arms, housing, intelligence, and other means of support to those fighters who took bigger risks than themselves. You can see, in this book mentioned above about the Dutch resistance, that it took some work for the underground to get itself armed properly to carry out their support of the allies who were coming to liberate them. The in-country citizens who were loyal to the rule of law and ran the resistance were a critical part of the allied operations.

Throughout Europe and the rest of Nazi or Imperial Japanese-occupied areas, people quickly learned that they had to keep the secret of their hidden weapons to themselves. The more people talked, the more they were discovered and locked up or killed.

If such a thing happens in America, what would be your role? If Democrats, Independents, Jews, and racial groups opposing a dictator were being systematically exterminated, what would you be doing? Was there a way to be neutral when fellow citizens were being rounded up and placed into concentration camps and exterminated by the millions during WWII? As much as we would like to think that nothing like this could ever happen in America, especially after WWII when we all fought to rid the earth of nationalism and the Nazi party and nationalists in Japan, January 6th suggests that this could repeat itself once again here in America.

You may have seen what seems to be a conflicting concept in this book. On one hand, I have said for you to keep your gun purchases secret. On the other hand, I have also said that if you acquire guns, then Trumpists will be less likely to attempt a coup again and install a dictatorship. One is individual, and the other is collective. Just because your individual gun purchase is private and not subject to public knowledge, if Democrats, Independents, and communities of color were getting guns and storing them in a big way, everyone would know it. Just like how we know who has been buying guns and arming themselves in the last decade, and why they have done so. In Jimmy Buffett's speak, this is what is called the "coconut telegraph." People always know, and journalists always find the story, but it will be collective and not individual. Everyone will know if there are millions of guns in the hands of a new group, but won't know whether you individually have one. Keep your gun purchases private for now.

CHAPTER TWENTY-THREE

SNITCHES GET STITCHES

One of comedian Trevor Noah's favorite sayings is: "Snitches get stitches, baby, that's what I'm talking about." I laugh every time he says it. You may think that this is just a joke, but on the street, it is a real thing. It means that informants get what they have coming – stitches. Informants are a despicable lot, usually criminals themselves, that is true, but I used them in police work all the time.

With that in mind, who can you trust with information about your home defense weapon or involvement in the resistance to restore democracy if this came to pass? Your best friends? Your family? Your local political organizations or associates? None of the above. The real world is very different. Most insurgencies against a dictatorship learn very quickly that loose lips do sink ships. Even a small amount of pressure will get many people telling everything they know. Some will provide information just to show that they were trusted with it in the first place. People love to blab "secret" information. It's just what humans do.

My partner and I, & Ted Dahm in a booking photo & Cessna 182
N7380S, which was later lost in a crash.

I used to teach classes on Advanced Narcotics Investigations
and Informant Development for the Washington State Criminal
Justice Training Commission and the United States Department
of Justice. I specialized in American, Mexican, and Columbian
organized crime drug investigations. American drug crime families are simple, and it is not difficult to turn informants from
within these groups. We did it all the time. Mexican crime families
used to be tough to break into but are not so today. Columbians
were the most difficult for everyone in law enforcement for a very
long time. They were smart. Before they hired you, they made you
fill out a job application listing every single extended relative you
had. If you turned informer, they assured you, they would hunt
down and kill all of them, just to send a message to others who
might think of doing the same.

One of the largest original cocaine smuggling organizations
in the Seattle area was run by a guy named Ted Dahm. That was
a very long time ago when cocaine was still new. He had a thriv-
ing business empire and was making lots of money, but his plan
had a catch. He had to drive to Los Angeles and back each week

with loads of cocaine. It was a bummer to be driving and traveling when he could have been using the cocaine and cash with his friends, enjoying a very high-priced lifestyle. We knew about him and his organization, and one day another detective and I hatched what we thought was a cool plan. One of the lowest guys on his payroll had a suspended driver's license and an extensive history of criminal traffic violations. His record was enough to put him in jail for a mandatory 90 days if he were caught driving. Generally, we couldn't flip an informant on such a chippy charge, but we also knew this guy had a phobia about jail, and he was a drug addict (which his boss did not know).

We arrested him while he was driving and told him about the 90-day jail term he was facing. He agreed to cooperate. Just like that. We asked him if he knew any criminals and he identified his boss, Ted Dahm, as a target. We acted surprised. We told him to tell his boss that he knew some pilots who were also crooks. My partner and I were both pilots. A couple of days later we got a call from Ted, and he asked us how much it would be to fly to LA and back. We gave him a price and he agreed. This was going to cut his travel time to LA and back by several days a week! Ted could not wait to have more fun in his spare time. It never dawned on him that a pilot might be a police detective. We ran this by our bosses, and they didn't see a problem with it.

It was a blast. Just in case we were hijacked, and the fact that we were so close to Mexico and did not want to get tortured, we carried no ID of any kind. We duct-taped two handguns under the dash of the plane up in the front. Our contingency plan, in case we were hijacked, was to fly around for a while and say we were lost, and then hand the bad guy a map and shoot him in the head with the gun concealed behind the map, shooting through the map. We figured that a bullet from either of our guns would go at such an angle that it would not hit any aircraft control devices in the tail and just go out the side of the plane after it went through his head. This was probably not the best idea in the world, but it seemed like a good idea at the time. We just knew that there was no way we were going to allow ourselves to get tortured in Mexico. We also had a secret code we could send using a radio transponder in the plane. If it were received by Air Traffic Control, the controllers would alert the military that something was wrong. They also had the numbers and codes to understand the message and to call our units back in Washington State and in California with further coded pre-arranged messages.

In the end, we flew Ted Dahm to California with $234,000.00 dollars in cash. He bought 10 kilograms of pure cocaine that was worth nearly a million dollars in street value. He also picked up a load of illegal gun silencers from a machine shop in the LA area. We arrested him in Los Angeles on our second trip with him and he was charged in Federal Court. This was a significant seizure of cocaine at the time. He was so shocked that his pilot "friends" were cops that he became catatonic for two days after finding out.

The point of this story is how easy it is to flip people and get them to inform against their friends, associates, and even their family members. Think about the risk this guy took. The driver informed against a criminal organization that would have been more than happy to kill him for doing so, just to avoid a driving violation and a little bit of local jail time. I could tell you hundreds of stories just like that one.

People swear they would never flip and inform on their friends, family, or associates, but they do it all the time. It is not that difficult to get someone to inform against others. There are countless motivations and psychological reasons for why it is so easy to do. The point is, if you are in such a situation someday in the future, the fewer people who know about your plans or involvement the better.

Ted Dahm's $234,000.00 in cash, ten kilograms of cocaine, firearms, and silencers.

I once arrested another guy, Randy Johnson, for running a drug enterprise who took an oath with his cohorts that they would all never tell on anyone in their group, even if they were having their fingernails pulled out one at a time. Sounds painful. We knew about the promise due to a phone intercept that happened when a digital phone recorder, or Pen Register, was being installed on their phone. We thought it was funny. It was a large group, and when I arrested Johnson and took him to the prosecutor's office for an interview, it only took 20 minutes before he was giving up everyone, including his own mother. She was part of his smuggling operation and made the trips from LA to Seattle in a Ford LTD because it had one of the largest trunks of any car at the time.

Most people think they are too tough to snitch until they are facing either legal pressure or personal gain. I can tell you that most people will do it. The only people who cannot inform against you are those who don't have any knowledge about you in the first place.

I can also tell you that a skillful investigator can get almost anyone to talk within about four hours of interrogation. I mean just polite discussion, not torture or any good-cop bad-cop stuff like you see on TV. Torture does not get reliable information, nor does too much pressure. A person under pressure or pain will tell you anything you want to hear in order to feel better. Good interrogators don't need it.

I also learned that a detective could get a person, in some cases, to admit to a crime he did not even commit. For that reason, professional police investigators and prosecutors will always require corroborating evidence before charging someone based on a confession alone.

My point here is that if you are going to join the resistance against a dictatorial regime, you should not tell people about it who do not absolutely need to know, maybe not even many of your own family members. Certainly not any friends or associates who are not among a very small number of highly trusted resistance members. These groups will be broken down into very small cells that do not know the identity of other ones. That will keep you, your weapon, and your involvement as secret and safe as possible.

By the time the "Troubles" came to an end in Northern Ireland, (1968-1998), it is widely reported that nearly half of the members of the IRA were providing information to their opponents. Even higher numbers in the leadership were cooperating with the British or Northern Ireland Governments. A couple of good books on this subject are *Say Nothing* by Patrick Radden Keefe (2019) and *Rebel Hearts* by Kevin Tollis (2015). Barrack Obama recommended *Say Nothing*, and it is an excellent read. The title comes from the concept that if you ever talk to any investigators at all, they will get everything from you over time. Hence the concept, "If you say anything, say nothing." If you think a dedicated person in a political cause would never inform, then read, *Killing Rage* by Eammon Collins (1998), who details how it happened to him. Another example is former Senator John McCain who was a prisoner of war in Vietnam. Senator McCain was a great American hero, but under the pressure of torture, he talked to those imprisoning him. Most people would. No one is immune. Keep a plan like this to yourself and do not tell others. No one can tell things about you that they do not know.

You might now ask when you should reveal what you have, whom to tell about it, and then how to use it if it becomes necessary. Good question. There isn't a simple answer, other than to say you will know it when the time comes. That is how these things work out. All voting and elections will have ended. Those not swearing loyalty to the regime will be arrested or "detained" and hauled off. Our judicial and legislative branches of government will be ended or compromised and not function independently. You and your friends will know what to do when the time comes, however, you should proceed with the utmost caution and deliberation until then.

November 10, 2017, Russian President Vladimir Putin, who very seldom smiles, with U.S. President Donald Trump. Alamy Stock Photo.

CHAPTER TWENTY-FOUR

O CANADA! &
WAR IN EUROPE

Our neighbor to the north published a report on November 27, 2019, on its official website called *Statistics Canada*, indicating the nation had 249 firearm-related homicides in 2018. Yet there are 34.7 firearms for each 100 Canadians in the nation. Canadians are familiar with firearms and have plenty of them, but they approach responsible firearm ownership differently than we do. America's firearm homicide rate per capita is almost triple that of Canada

Canada has its own problems of course, as all countries do. But what is happening in America is now spilling over into Canada, as evidenced by truckers in February of 2022 who blocked routes from Canada to the US, causing hundreds of millions of dollars of damage to both economies. These illegal rioters flew Trump and confederate flags and were even openly supported by some far-right American politicians like U.S. Senator Ted Cruz.

Dwayne Lich went to court in Canada and told the Canadian Judge at his wife's bail hearing that he and his arrested wife were just exercising their "First Amendment rights" to which the judge responded, "Your what?" The first amendment to the Canadian constitution says: *"An Act to amend and continue the Act 32-33 Victoria chapter 3; and to establish and provide for the Government of the Province of Manitoba, 1870, 33 Vict., c. 3 (Can.)"*. In other words, that Canadian had never read the Canadian constitution and didn't realize that the American Constitution does not apply to Canada. Espousing "First Amendment Rights" as a justification for committing crimes will not protect anyone arrested in Canada, let alone in the United States.

Two recent stories out of Canada show how destabilizing the ascendency of Trump and his nationalists are, and how the events of January 6th are impacting everyone. One is a book by Canadian author Stephen Marche called *The Next Civil War: Dispatches from the American Future.* He is asking Canadians to begin thinking of what it will be like when democracy ends in America and how this will impact Canada. The other is an op-ed is by Thomas

Homer-Dixon called *The American Polity is cracked and might collapse. Canada must prepare.* He is the Director of the Cascade Institute, a think tank. It was published in the Canadian newspaper, the *Globe and Mail.* It begins by suggesting that American democracy could collapse, causing extreme domestic political instability and widespread civil violence.

Both writers predicted that on our current course, democracy is likely coming to an end in America in the not-too-distant future. They also predict that a second American Civil War is now likely. The question for them is what to do if a Trumpian dictatorship begins demanding that Americans who oppose Trump be returned from Canada to America for punishment or even death. What will Canada do in such a case? How can they defend their democracy when ours unravels? What will they do to help Americans reclaim our democratic republic in such a case?

While I was drafting this book, Russia's Putin was massing troops and weapons on the border of Ukraine. The world held its breath in hopes that an invasion would not take place. Sadly, the invasion is underway, and for the first time in 77 years, Europe is now on the precipice of a world war. Not since the rise of Nazism and Adolph Hitler has anything on the potential of this scale occurred. There have been wars in Europe, and people in the Balkans (the general area of Albania, Bosnia and Herzegovina, Bulgaria, Croatia, Kosovo, Montenegro, North Macedonia, Romania, Serbia, and Slovenia) can attest to wars and genocide, but not since Hitler marched into Poland on September 1, 1939, has anything like this happened. Putin has threatened nuclear war if opposition to his efforts to overtake eastern Europe goes too far.

Most of the world responded in shock, dismay, and condemnation against Russia and Putin for this war of conquest. But right after the invasion began, Donald Trump called Putin a "genius" for invading Ukraine and said that Putin could take the country "for only $2.00 in sanctions." He urged Putin that this was a bargain. He also called the United States stupid and dumb. Trump later tried to correct some of his pro-Putin statements, but in the first few days, he expressed his true feeling for Putin and the invasion of Ukraine. In the past, Trump offered his support for Putin's invasion of Crimea by saying that the people living there were better off being ruled by Russia, even though this was sovereign Ukrainian territory.

During his term, Trump tried to extort Ukraine by withholding military aid that the U.S. had promised Ukraine unless the country produced evidence of wrongdoing by Hunter Biden. Biden is the son of President Joe Biden, who was just a candidate opposing Trump at the time. Trump's delaying of weapons to Ukraine in 2019 and 2020 damaged Ukraine's ability to defend against a Russian invasion, including this one in February of 2022.

Without Putin's massive and illegal internet disinformation campaign, Trump would have never been elected. The Department of Justice Special Prosecutor report by former FBI Director, Robert Muller, said that Russian interference in the 2016 election on behalf of Trump was "sweeping and systemic." After studying the reports of investigations into the matter, I believe that the Trump campaign operatives were meeting and coordinating with the Russian disinformation campaign. As a result of the special counsel investigation, 34 people were indicted, although Trump himself has not been charged with a crime. During that period, Trump mused that Putin might be his best friend, and as recently as March of 2022, in a tape-recorded conversation with John Daly said, "You know, he was a friend of mine. I got along great with him."

Trump spent his four years in office doing everything he could to demonize, underfund, and undermine NATO, the North

Atlantic Treaty Organization created after WWII to restrain the menace of the Union of Soviet Socialist Republics, dominated by Russia. Trump has made it clear how much he admires Putin personally and Trump's wish to be a ruler in Putin's style.

So, here's why this all matters to Americans who are considering acquiring weapons to help preserve the American democratic republic. What is happening in Ukraine now is what dictators will do every time if they do not face the restraints of the democratic rule of law. If you want to know what a Trumpian dictatorship will look like in America when our democracy is gone, look at Russia and the war and suffering in Ukraine today. WWII in Europe was the direct result of the rise of fascism and the Nazis taking power. It is now a war crime in Russia for journalists or citizens to report on the fact that there is a war or to criticize Putin in public. People opposing Putin will receive 15-year prison sentences and go to work camps, or worse.

When Trump was president, how many times did you hear him say that free and fair reporting by the media was fake news? How many times did you hear him talk about wishing he could get rid of the free press as Putin has in Russia? In a March 8, 2022, interview with Trump's former press sectary, Stephanie Grisham on *The View*, she said, "Trump admired Putin for just being able to kill journalists or whoever."

If America falls to fascism, I fear for Canada and other democracies as well. They have good reason to be deeply concerned about a dictatorial regime in America. Putin is but a current example of how dictators always attempt to expand their borders. I suspect that if Trumpists ever took total power in America, they would try to expand America's boundaries. Mainstream news organizations in other countries are now watching our potential decline with deep concern.

Trumpism is a belief system. It is not about just the man. Trump simply gave voice to white supremacists, anti-Semitics, and other radical nationalists who seek to end democracy and replace it with a dictatorship without constitutional restraints. There are plenty of others who are willing and able to lead this movement if Trump were gone or discarded.

Simply put, democracy is in peril. If given another chance at what they tried to do on January 6, 2021, Trumpists will not repeat the same mistakes again. They might be successful next time if we do not stop them before they get the chance.

CHAPTER TWENTY-FIVE

A THOUSAND
EASY PIECES

Y ou may feel that as a country, we need to do more to protect our citizens from improper gun use and violence. I agree. Curiously, so do most gun owners in America. Although support for more stringent gun laws will tend to ebb and flow, depending on the media coverage of mass shootings, most gun owners believe that safety should be a higher priority. A handful of common sense and minimally invasive regulations could make all the difference in the world for everyone involved on both sides of the gun control debate. Then why is it so difficult?

Powerful gun lobbying interests, political leaders, and some conservative religious groups are usually able to keep common-sense gun regulations from happening in any effective way. Gun safety is not a gun rights issue at all, but it has been made into a political and fundraising one. If you terrify people that their rights are about to be taken away, you can get them to vote and give money to causes that are often against their own self-interest. If some leaders can keep Americans terrified and thinking from a position of fear, then no practical, logical, or fact-based discussion can be undertaken. Radicalized people cannot participate in logical discussions. That is how their leaders want them to be. Fear sells, and it delivers votes and lots of cash to those peddling it.

This is also an era of people spewing their hate anonymously. Anonymity makes hate so easy today. There are talkers, bullies, and cowards. Not that long ago, cowardly racist members of the KKK wore hooded masks to hide their identity when committing their crimes. The anonymity of the internet today has a similar type of mask for many people espousing racist, fascist, and anti-Semitic views. But I feel that anonymous people have nothing worth listening to. Mark Twain once said, "A mob of cowards has no sand in the presence of a man known to be splendidly brave and can easily be defeated by a single courageous person." (He used the word "sand" to describe personal courage, a common term in writing of that age.)

The day could be coming when you may need to find courage in yourself. It's there inside you. So do it in public. Ahead of the Second Amendment is the First Amendment: *"Congress shall make no law respecting an establishment of religion, or prohibiting the free exercise thereof; or abridging the freedom of speech, or of the press; or the right of the people peaceably to assemble, and to petition the Government for a redress of grievances."* Americans should step up on the soapbox and state their opinion in full view of everyone else who knows exactly who they are.

Plenty of people will criticize my comments, but Winston Churchill once said, "You will never get to your destination if you stop and throw rocks at every dog that barks at you along the way." I love that quote. Let there be critics, I don't really care. Let them bark. Parotitic Americans need to stand up and speak the truth, but in public, and not from the shadows.

There is still time to protect our democracy, but you need to get involved. Make sure you vote while you still can. Make sure everyone you know votes. Protest and oppose all efforts to limit or in any way impede voting or votes being counted. Keep informed and get engaged in educating people about the danger of militant nationalists trying to take over our country. Don't buy into political hype from any side. Search diligently for facts that can be verified, not just reading, or watching ideas that upset you without any foundation.

Not all people who disagree with you are evil. Respect others and try to learn more about them. Even Winston Churchill, who rightly wanted to kill all Nazi nationalists during WWII, felt that the allies should at least try to fix some of the fixable ones. Try to listen and learn from those who may not be too far gone yet. Try to find common ground with people who are not yet fascists or Nazis, but in the end, don't be foolish and fail to prepare in case all of this goes very wrong.

You might want to think of gun ownership in some of these scenarios as a safe, secure, rainy-day fund against fascists and Nazis, not a credit card for your ego as many Americans do today.

I also want to point out that I have told the true police and combat stories in this book to show you what I see and how I understand what can happen when things go wrong in tactical situations. Most things in my police career went fine, but those stories do not carry a lesson. I am alive today despite the mistakes that I and others made. Some occurred because of my own errors and misjudgments. Not everything I did was a good idea at times, nor have I shared everything with you in this book. I used these stories to help you understand that making mistakes or being incautious, as I have been at times, can have deadly consequences for us to learn from.

Finally, you might remember the concept of "inevitable discovery" described earlier in this book. It was inevitable that someday a physicist would discover that a neutron going into an unstable atom of Uranium 235 would force two neutrons out, which led to atomic bombs, and finally the hydrogen bomb, something that could end all higher forms of life on earth. What has kept us from doing this, so far anyway, is a principle of deterrence called "Mutual Assured Destruction" or MAD for short. The idea is that no one power can use its weapons because the resulting retaliation would be so unthinkable that no one would win. Everyone would be dead at the end of the exchange. Trump supporters plan on their Civil War being successful without much fighting or bloodshed, just like Hitler as he rose to power. They know that they currently have guns, and you don't. If millions of responsible people who do not have guns today, got and kept them safely, this would change the equation. They would be deterred. Their Trumpian dictatorship would come at a high cost, one they might not be willing to pay.

ACKNOWLEDGMENTS

I published my first book in August of 2021, called *Climbing Kilimanjaro With Africa's Top Guide by Erick Kivelege*. Erick was my partner on that project. That book is now available on Amazon around the world. What I learned on my first book project was how many people are needed in a successful book project.

Like the Kili Book, this book also required the input of many people, from police work, the military, political leaders, educators, historians, and interested folks who shared their ideas, questions, opinions, and in some cases, their fears. It is customary to name and thank the people who spent hours being interviewed, helping with research, editing, or formatting a book, but this case is different. No one wanted to be named here in the acknowledgment section. They were all very supportive of the concept of this book and its being published, but they did not want to take the risk of having their names printed here because they agree with the lessons of this book, such as "If you say something, say nothing." I understand, but thank them all, anonymously, all the same – they know who they are, and I really appreciate all their hard work and encouragement. I would also say that this response to having their names in this section is one last warning on where our country is today. These are troubling times.

Also Available on Amazon today from Christopher Hurst:

Climbing Kilimanjaro With Africa's Top Guide
by Erick Kivelege

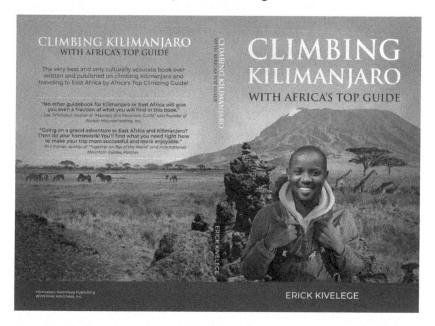

For decades, people traveling to East Africa have had to rely on guidebooks that have been written from a western or even a colonial point of view. Most of these books make mention of African savages being tamed by missionaries and lands being discovered and conquered by explorers. It's long past time for these old concepts to be put to rest and replaced with the true history of this remarkable land. This is the very best and only culturally accurate guidebook ever written and published on climbing Kilimanjaro and traveling to East Africa by Africa's Top Climbing Guide! No matter if you are a traveler, an armchair reader of exciting outdoor adventures, or just want to know the true story of East Africa, this book has it all. Here is a message from Erick on our book:

"For the very first time, here is the true story of Kilimanjaro and East Africa. As a Certified Climbing Guide, I have summited Kilimanjaro over 500 times. I was born and raised here in Moshi Town, Tanzania. I know this land, it's culture, and our people. This is a place of mystery and wonder like no other on earth. Past guide-books by Westerners and Europeans can't give you even a fraction of what you will find in the pages of this book. They could never understand this land or Kilimanjaro as I do. Asante Sana (thank you!) for buying this book. I will welcome you on your journey of a lifetime to my homeland of East Africa and Kilimanjaro!"

You can buy it on Amazon today! We also sometimes have a limited number of copies on sale at https://www.kutembea publishing.com depending on inventory.

Made in USA - Kendallville, IN
54686_9780578361611
04.12.2022 1625